ANYTHING
FOR A DEAL

I'll get the keys, sir. Tee hee hee.

ANYTHING FOR A DEAL

David Glazebrook

AMHERST

ISBN 1 903637 18 X

Printed in Great Britain

First published in 2003 by

Amherst Publishing Limited
Longmore House, High Street, Otford, Sevenoaks, Kent TN14 5PQ

If you ever want to achieve anything, don't put it off. Don't think to yourself, 'I'd love to have gone for that', but didn't have the bottle to go ahead and reach that goal.

While you're reading this, have one thought. Like history, the newspapers once wrote that behind all good men, world leaders, is a strong woman giving that man a push. Well, I'm not a world leader - my cupboard's under lock and key - but I've got the best wife, no, the world's best wife. She's a friend, a great drinking partner, and the one who gave me that push.

For Jackie - love you, thanks.

Contents

1

The Salesman

Those summer breaks - how many of you go on your holidays to the sunny Mediterranean? I know thousands do each year, whether you go to the south of France, sunny Spain, or sun-drenched beaches on the Algarve.

Basically, anywhere on the tourist holiday spots, you'll be hounded by those wonderful people - the time-share reps, the ones who wait on every street corner for their unsuspecting clients to fall in to their trap. If anything is going free, sure enough, people want to see what's on offer. These reps are out every day during the summer months, touting for you to go and view the complex and all its wonderful apartments. They mention a free meal, bottle of spirits, tickets to the water fun park. So you go along to see the place and what they have to offer.

The man you meet there in his shirt and tie, is the salesman. He is going to sell you a dream. Remember, you don't have to buy anything - you have just come along to view.

The next thing you know, two and a half hours have gone by. You've been bored out of your skull, listening to what this company representative presented to you, when all you wanted was the freebies. Two and a half hours when you could have been out in the sun getting those rays for which you came on holiday. People work hard all year for those nice relaxing weeks away to chill out and unwind.

So can anyone tell me why people want to sit in a room with the sweltering heat of the Mediterranean sun for a couple of hours when they could be sight-seeing, swimming or drinking. Who in their right mind wants to buy an apartment for one week in the year for some ridiculous price, never to own the flat, and then have to pay ground rent as well. So you are the unlucky one who got roped into purchasing a room - and you have to phone up to see when you can use it. When you see a complex with two hundred rooms, it makes you wonder. That salesman just ruined your holiday. Don't they get aggressive when you say no and want to leave? His boss is going to want to know why you've left without buying that apartment. He's just doing his job, and he has eight months to make his money. He's a hard-selling salesman and, once you're hooked, you have to go along with his spiel - it's hard to get away from.

So whenever you go shopping to buy a car, electrical goods, double glazing, insurance, or even a mortgage, you will meet the person we all hate. The individual who has your best interest at heart - the salesman, or salesperson. They couldn't give a toss about you. They're only interested in reaching their targets.

2

The Chosen Trade

The stories in this book are all based on real-life events in the motor trade. The names of the salesmen, the showrooms, and their location, have been changed to protect their true identities.

If I could sit down with a friend for a chat of an evening, I can guarantee by the end of the night we would be crying with laughter at some of the episodes that we recall from past events.

So why do so many people get into this trade?

Is it their good looks? No.

Able to listen to what people want? No.

Clean teeth, fresh breath? No, but it helps.

Cheap after shave? Yes.

Smart dress and pride in their appearance, hair well-groomed (no dandruff showing, no cats, dogs, or lovers' long hair on the suit jacket).

Enough bullshit to fill a yard skip. Shut up when bored.

There's the salesman who wants to give it away, the man who likes to build up a rapport with anyone just to give it as a freebie - if it moves, discount it.

Like most sales reps, we all want to be the best the company has ever had, win those prizes, like the legendary Tommy Smith, who could sell 40-50 cars a month with a percentage on the strap (finance). He would take home three grand a month plus what ever bonus was going, win whatever competition they held, like two weeks holiday, a test drive around the race circuit, Rolex watches. That's who we all want to be like.

Do we hell! Give me the flash car to show my mates, the car I'm going to pull the birds with, petrol, money in my bin at the end of each month. Sell cars, hit your target - that's all you have to do to earn that bonus. You're in the money, what a good job. You get to meet the rich and the famous (that reminds me - someone owes me a rugby shirt). Deliver a car to some weird and wonderful places.

But then there's the other side to the trade - the not so rich and famous - the people you sell anything to. You give them the dream of how they're going to look, feel, what their friends are going to think of their new car. But, at a cost. They'll work out your finance for you and tell you how much you are going to spend per month - not how much you can afford.

Each main dealership's showrooms are different. There's the gin palace made up of glass, with garage workshop, M.O.T bays, valeting area, normally has one of each model in the showroom, all polished waiting for you to sit inside. Picture yourself driving down the motorway, those country lanes, that pub - yes sir, madam, this is you, take the car for a drive, feel the car. Seventy used cars on the forecourt, no more then three years old, fairly priced up. A ladies and gentlemen's toilets, television area, playthings for the children, the showroom laid out to the manufacturer's specification, the background music, the tables, even the drinks machine is what they have laid down. Finance is done through a finance house which just does vehicles, the interest rate usually a percent higher - no more so they can compete with the banks. If you don't like the way it is, you lose the franchise.

Showroom two - the used car specialist - cars bought from auction, slightly high in miles but with a service history, normally just before they need an M.O.T. Mainly deal with finance companies whose rate is higher than any bank, please, when selling cars, no bonuses, but the targets are realistic. The owner is always around so that's added pressure to sell cars, might have fifty cars, the odd people carrier, four by fours, vans, anything to bring the money in. The showroom has three sales desks, two or three cars in the building valeting bay, workshop with two or three ramps plus an M.O.T. bay. Kettle for hot drinks, no children's play area, no television.

Then there's back-street Billy. His cars are the ten or twenty-year-old, worn-out wrecks, two hundred and fifty pounds worth of cars, that only a north London taxi driver would buy. If you ever want a cheap car, this is the man for you. It might have an M.O.T. with six months left on it, it might not. It will not have road tax. Reading the signs, for sale, good runner, one owner, low mileage, clean car.

This car is normally red or white - it's a good runner: it's had a new battery. One owner: that means it's an ex-taxi cab. Low mileage: been around the clock twice. Clean car: it's been brushed out, washed and cleaned - normally sold as seen - what you see is what you get - once it's gone, you don't bring it back.

The street trader who puts his cars that he has for sale, near or opposite a showroom, leaves a phone number in the window, so you think that it has something to do with showroom nearby. It hasn't. How it works: customers go on to the forecourt, don't see any cars they like, eye up the cars over the road from the showroom. They know a friend who needs a cheap car so they phone him up, mention to him what they've seen.

He comes down, has a look over the car then phones the number on the window. The bloke arrives five minutes later. They shake hand, he parts with his money, he's then given the keys and the log book and off he goes on his travels - deal done. The showroom has just lost a potential customer.

The finance showroom has no forecourt, no television, no M.O.T. bay - no meeting the customers here, no showing them around the cars. No, this is all achieved over the telephone. Getting the customer in is a priority. As long as they can walk, you get them in. If you have county court judgements against you and don't like paying back anything you borrow, they'll help you get a car, but it will cost you.

The car supermarket, with hundreds of cars all waiting to go, and at a reasonable price, in fact cheaper than the main dealers on some cars, so there's always competition out there for you to buy a car.

Well there you have it - a rough guide to the showrooms or portacabins. Remember, if you want a car and you know what vehicle you require, spare a thought for that person who sits at the other side of the desk. What is he or she going to go through to get you your car on time?

Every person who walks on to the forecourt, or comes into the showroom, is a pound sign. Someone who pays for my night out, the curry on a Saturday night, the beer and the wine. The company's money pays the home bills. So when a Billy Bunter (a punter) wants to buy a car, I'll be there for them.

The more cars I flog, the quicker my credit cards get paid, so two cars a day keeps the P45 away. Then, if I get pissed off with the dealership, it's time to move on, go and work for a rival main dealer. I'm here for myself when there's a deal. I'll make sure it's me dealing it. I hate seeing other salesmen dealing it when it should be me. Me, I'm Mr Greedy.

It started years ago, when I went for an interview for a job as a salesman. The only thing I ever sold was pints of beer in a pub. That was easy, that's what the customer wanted. The only mats were beer mats with logos on, saying, 'have a cold one for the road'.

So when I saw an advert: sales executive wanted, good salary, hours to suit, good benefits, I gave the said phone number a call to see what it's all about. I explained that I liked meeting people and enjoyed a challenge.

I went to the interview and had a chat with this guy. He went on about how good his company was - talk about blowing your own trumpet - that it was an up and coming dealership. He told me how good they were and how well they treat their staff. That was on a Thursday. I started with them on the following Monday. That should have told me something.

I found out a week later what the hell I'd done, then spent six months trying to leave...

3

The First Monday - The Site

Dressed in my wedding suit, not a hair out of place, I'm off to catch the train with a one way ticket. I'll be driving home in my company car - all a bit exciting, I must say. So with my driving licence, lunch box, mobile phone, money for my fare to the train station, off I go.

Thinking about it, I haven't been up this early for years. The last time I'm sure was when I was being sick once. The train leaves for London at 6.45 - that's early! So with ten minutes to go, I grab a lift to town and to the station. Passing four dealerships on the way, thinking to myself, that's where I want to be in a few years time - just five minutes from home - but first we need some experience.

It has been ages since I've caught a train to London. I'd forgotten what it was like. All I know is that by the time we get to Lewisham we're all going to feel like sardines crammed in a tin. Now I know how those animals feel when they're being transported around Europe. By the time the train had got to Waterloo, my carriage was heaving with bodies. The cattle crossing the continent are treated better than these people. I couldn't do this every day for a living.

My station - Waterloo - it's time to leave the crowd. So, I'm jumping off the train looking for the exit. There it is - up the flight of steps along the gangway. To find my connection, I go up along the corridor to where a sign indicates the way to trains to the west. To the left and down the small flight of steps, on to the large foyer. You could have a field day here if you're a train spotter. Euro star, the train to Paris and Belgium, is over there to my right, and platform 10 is where my connection is waiting. The journey should take twenty minutes. Off the train goes, past Vauxhall and the Kennington oval, over the River Thames. I can see the London Eye - not a nice day to go up there today. It's very overcast and I suppose we will get rain some time today. Past Clapham junction, the busiest station in England, and we arrive at my destination. I remembered I had been here before some ten years ago. I was helping a builder friend out, putting up a ceiling. This brings back memories - there is a boat race here once a year between two universities.

The walk from this station should take ten minutes, or so I was told. They said they couldn't send anyone out to meet me because they were short of staff, so I didn't mind the walk. I suppose I need to familiarise myself with this area. Old Victorian houses lined the route - not much room to park if you own a car around here.

What a pleasant walk - a space to play football and

walk the dog over to my left. The smell of boiled cabbage hung in the air. There must be a brewery nearby - what a stench - it seems to be getting stronger as I'm walking towards Wandsworth.

Well, here we are at the forecourt. Access into the showroom is a little further up the path. With all its flags and bunting along the rails, it must be there to encourage people to come in and see what's inside. On the forecourt, there must be forty or fifty cars, different shapes and sizes, with a variety of colour every other car.

Here is the showroom, which looks like an old builders' merchant yard. It must have been built just after the second world war - it looks well dated for a dealership. I go up to the reception area, with no receptionist.

'Can I help?' a voice called out.

'I'm here to see a Brian Fulmer, the sales manager,' I replied.

'OK, he should be around here somewhere. Let me find him for you. What's your name?'

'Chris Maynard.'

'Just wait there a moment, Chris. Brian, you have a young man to see you,' he called out on the speaker phone.

A couple of minutes later, the manager turned up in the showroom.

'Hello Chris, and welcome,' Brian said, stretching out his hand. 'I hope you enjoy your stay with us.' We shook hands.

'Sorry I'm late. That walk was a bit longer than I thought.'

'Don't worry about that. You're not late. Well, welcome

to Browns. I'll give you a rundown of the place. What we are here is a satellite unit for a main dealership. We can sell any car we like - the new cars in the showroom are on show so people can take them for test drives. We can sell them, but you can buy them cheaper from the main dealer. We stick to selling used cars, but if we sell a new car, we have had a result. Let me introduce you to the rest of the sales team, when we can find them. We have had a good weekend - we sold about twenty cars. The weekend starts Friday afternoon till Sunday afternoon, so Monday is going to be a busy day for those who sold anything. There's loads of money to be made here once you know what you're doing, Chris.

'This way. I'll show you around - through the sliding doors out on to the forecourt. As you can see, each row contains ten cars.'

'How many vehicles do you have on this site?'

'Between fifty and sixty used cars, plus those new cars. The stock is rotating all the time. The target is 120 cars to be sold a month. I don't think that's a lot for four salesmen, and once you've settled in I reckon we will be hitting that target every month. Once we achieve that, we get a good bonus from the owner of the company. Let's start here, Chris. If your customer is buying a car, and the customer has a part exchange, you bring their car appraisal form to this office here. This place here is our underwriters, pointing to the flat-roofed building. They will value the vehicle - the price of what the car is worth. That's the easy part, so when a car is sold we put it in this area here, set aside for sold cars. If it needs any work, it has to go into the workshop which is over there. This is the service area. Every car here we try and put a little profit on to it, so if it does require some work it comes out of that. Those thieving bastards will try and take most of it out so we're left with a small profit, so watch them.

'This way, please, to the service reception. As you can see, people are booking their vehicles in for some work. It could be for M.O.T. or a general service, so we will come back to them later. This counter is for the parts department. Ring this bell and an idiot will appear. Ding dong, no answer, again ding dong (I'm busy). Like I said, an idiot will appear. Get here, you fat twat. Ah, good morning Del, have a nice Sunday off?'

'Not bad, Brian, but I'm back here.'

'Anyway, meet Chris, our new sales executive.'

'Hi mate, any problems, I'll help you out.'

'Rip off, more like.'

'Cheers mate.'

'Come on, Chris, he has had a delivery so we'll go back to the workshop.'

Back at the counter. 'Hi Jez, good morning to you.'

'Brian, did you have a good weekend?'

'If you call one day off, a weekend, yes, I had a great weekend. Meet Chris, he's a new member of our crew here to sell loads of cars and make himself pot loads of gold.'

'Enjoy your stay here, Chris, talk to you later, mate. As you can see, I'm the only person who works here.'

'All right if I show him around?'

'Sure.'

'This way, Chris. As you can see, we have four ramps

although we really need five with the amount of work out there. This place is a licence to print money. I'd hate to bring my wife's car here. I'd be paying for ever. The price of their labour charges, but if the motorist's car needs the work, they have to bring it here.'

'Brian, I have to ask this question. I notice you have hardly any English-speaking staff working here for this garage - not being rude,' I said quietly, not wanting to be overheard.

'Chris, they all live locally. We just can't get the decent mechanics for the wages they want to pay. It's a multi-cultural society garage. We have Spanish, Russian, and I'm sure we have a few boat people. Around here they work for peanuts. It goes on in certain parts of London. No doubt we will have immigration officers paying us a visit soon.

'Right this way, through this door, and we are back on the forecourt. Now you get the picture. All these cars need to be sold, that's why we have taken you on. I know you have the makings of a good salesman. You just sell the cars at the price we give you. If they want finance, you have to introduce them to the business manager and he will sort out their terms and conditions. If a finance deal goes through, you get commission on that deal as well - that's about 5% which on a good month can be very good.'

'Where is the finance manager? Is he in today?'

'Jim, he will be in about 10 o'clock. He goes down to the west country where he has a house and a girlfriend. Remember, he is here to help you as well as himself. Chris, this is our showroom.'

As we walk up to the main entrance, through the door to the left is the receptionist. She will answer the phone to any sales calls, and pass them to the sales team in that order so everyone gets an equal share of the calls - that's fair. To the right was a two-tier showroom, three new cars down on the lower section, four cars on the upper. At the back of the showroom was a meeting room, then the business manager's room, and next to that was the sales manager's room, whilst the toilet was in the corner.

On my desk, I had a phone, a diary, and a notepad. A chrome-framed chair with a blue cushion to sit on, and a back rest. In front, there were two chairs for the customers, almost the same, but they had armrests (it was very fashionable in the early seventies). Three drawers: one for my mobile phone, the second drawer was for my sandwiches and newspaper. The lower drawer was for used enquiry sheets, the ones you don't want to follow up on, and used appraisal forms plus the rest of the company's junk.

The view from here was a block of flats, the penthouse type, a piece of land for exercising the dog, and the River Thames with trees lining the route, plus a footpath. No doubt I'll take a walk along there sometime. Directly in front of my desk, where I would be sitting, was another salesman's desk with one in front of him - no privacy here - looks like we can overhear each other when we are on the phone. I suppose I had the edge because I could see who came onto the forecourt first, being on the top level. We'll see. I noticed a silver car park up. Out stepped a bloke, no taller than five foot two and plump, a small

French general with no hair. He turns and locks his car, then makes his way towards the showroom. Through the open door he comes.

'Good morning, Mr Dobson,' said a voice from the reception area, followed by a grunt in reply as he made his way up the steps.

'Morning Terry, morning Sanjay.'

'Morning Jim,' both salesmen said in tandem.

My turn. 'Good morning,' I said, stretching out my hand. 'My name is Chris Maynard, new sales executive.'

'New sales guy, and how many cars are you going to sell this month, twenty, twenty five?'

'I'll give it a go,' I replied.

'No, you'll sell twenty to twenty-five cars. If not, you can fuck off out the doors and don't come back. Other than that, good morning to you Chris, I hope you enjoy your stay at this place of honour. Oh, by the way, I don't shake hands until you've sold your first cars.'

What a pratt, he was short, fat, had no hair, and thick rimmed glasses. Jumped-up prick in a suit. Well that's a nice way to start to get to like somebody.

'So, Chris, get out there and start selling some cars.'

'It's all right, Chris, he's winding you up. You're new here, his bit of power,' explained Brian. 'He's an ex-copper who got kicked out of the service, doesn't know how to handle people, can't get used to being in a different environment. Don't worry, you'll be all right. He needs you, you don't need him. If we have a good month, he is happy giving his ex-wife some of his wages.'

Sitting down at my desk again, I was wondering what

the fuck I had let myself in for. Staring out the window, the view seemed worse than before. Christ, have I really got to sell all those cars.

'It's all right mate, I had the same when I joined the company. He's like it every Monday morning. You'll find out when you've been here for a while. My name's Terry, by the way, been in the motor trade for twenty odd years. Been at some good dealerships, been at some shit holes as well. I've been here eighteen months now, so it ain't that bad.' Shaking my hand, he asked, 'Been in the trade long?'

'My first car sales job, mate, sold windows before this. My partner said, "go and have a try at selling cars". Saw an ad, now I'm here.'

'You'll soon get the hang of it,' said Terry. 'You can make a load of money selling cars in the right place. I won't scare you off, just enjoy yourself, they're all fucking muppets here. A word of advice, when you put your worksheet in on a car that's gone to have some work done to it, watch out for them in the service area. Those bastards will rip you off, so will the mechanics. Remember, the profit you make on the car when you sell it adds up for you to get a good bonus each month, but once it goes into the garage they will try their hardest to nick it from you.

'I was a gamekeeper before I came into this trade. I lived in Hampshire, lost that job when my boss died. The eldest son sold up so I had to leave the tied cottage. I moved in with a mate who was selling some old shitters from a little yard near the coast. He had a spare room above his office so I stayed there. Took up a sponge and a bucket, washed a few of his cars for him for a bit of money, next I was selling cars. He paid a hundred quid for every car I sold. I was selling twenty cars a month, getting cash in hand. I was laughing. The more I sold, the more money I made. It wasn't long before I bought a house and had money in the bank. That was twenty odd years ago. There's not many places like that left nowadays. People want warranties and free insurance and free services on the car now. They don't want to spend fuck all on the upkeep of their cars. They'll try and knock you down - they'll want you to take five hundred pounds off the screen price, then throw in free mats and a tank of petrol. Just let it go over your head like David Seaman. He lets things go over his head - it's a bit hard to make a living nowadays.'

'But he was our number one goalkeeper.'

'Who for, Arsenal?'

'No, England.'

'Do you follow any team, Terry?' I ask.

'Only the best in the world.'

'Oh, Man United, have you seen them play?'

'F'ing right. When they're in London, I make a point of going to watch them.'

'What about you, Chris, do you follow football?'

'No, I follow cricket. I sometimes play, but mainly watch nowadays. Oh, and rugby.'

'Well, Twickenham is only up the road, in fact quite a few rugby teams are around here. Posh area is this,' Terry said.

'I try and get to an evening game when summer comes.'

'There are also some good pubs around here, some along the river.'

'The trouble with that is I'll be getting home late, then be accused of having an affair. I have a jealous girlfriend who will phone me up if I am ten minutes overdue - half an hour and she will have the police looking for me. I remember being in a pub once, trying to get a job off this bloke. She called me on my mobile phone. I told her where I was but forgot to turn my phone off. She was there in five minutes and smacked me in the mouth for not taking her there. She was a psycho. Too right I'll go for a drink, starting from tonight.'

'I can see you're going to settle in here, mate.'

4

The First Deal

There's a yell from the receptionist, 'Sales enquiry for you, Chris.'

'Hello and good morning, my name is Chris, how may I help you?'

'I was just going through the local paper and noticed you have a fourteen hundred Escort in dark red. Can you tell me about it, please.'

'Sure, what's your name, sir?'

'Richard.'

'OK, Richard, it's a fourteen hundred, five-door, and priced at, let me see, on an X reg. One sec, Richard, I'll go and find out a bit more about the car for you.'

'OK.'

Finding out that we had a printout of all the cars really helped. I told him all about the car, how many owners, the service history, and the mileage on the car. 'So, did you want to test drive the car sometime today?'

'Say two o'clock this afternoon.'

'That's fine, Richard, can I just have a contact number in case something crops up? It's only for my reference. Do you know how to get here?'

'Sure, I pass the showroom all the time, oh my number.' He told me his number and I set too.

'Someone tell me what I have to do now. I have a guy coming down for a test drive.'

'You need to get the car ready. Make sure you've juice (petrol) in the car, and trade plates. Where is the car parked? If it's not in one of the aisles, you'll have to get it out so just make sure it's ready for sale,' Terry shouted.

The time - let's see, it's elevenish - time to find where the car is. That's handy, right on the end of the row. Right now, let's find out where they hide the keys, must be in that box on the wall. Here we are, all these bloody car keys look the same, all have yellow tags. (I love talking to myself).

Lets see - they all have the registration numbers and car colour on the tags, should make it a bit easier to find the one. Right, got it, now let's look to see if there's any petrol in the tank. In we get, let's start this baby up. Started first time, can't be bad. Right, let's park it in the bay by the wall, so when the bloke arrives, all I need to do is put the trade plates on and off we go, job done.

Ten to two, a man arrived with a woman, can't be his girlfriend, she is too old for that. Making their way to reception, my phone rings. 'Richard Clarke to see you,' the receptionist said.

'OK, I'm on my way.' Grabbing my jacket, I made my

way down to my customer.

'Hi, I'm Chris, you must be Richard. Thank you for coming, please follow me.' I lead them back towards my desk. 'It's been nice out, I can't believe it, it's been warm all day, summer has finally arrived. Please take a seat, let's see, do you have your driving licence on you?'

'Yes.'

'That's for the insurance. Would you like a tea or coffee?'

'Oh, no thank you.'

'I just have to get the trade plates, then we are ready for the off. Is your mother going to come with us?'

'No thanks, I'll stay here, I don't like the roads around London.'

'OK then, Richard, this way to the car. I don't know the roads round here so we'll drive around the block. Right let's go, here's the keys, the car is parked just over by the wall.' Seat belts on, mirror adjusted, he starts the car, and for my first test drive, let's begin. We head left out of the gates.

'Just go with the flow of the traffic. There's a rail bridge about a mile and a half up the road. If you turn left there, the side road will take us to the upper Richmond road, do a left at the junction at the end of the road, left again back along this road. Should take about twenty minutes, all depends on the traffic so enjoy the drive of your life. Sorry, that's a Peugeot saying, this is a Ford. Can I just say I'm not a driving instructor, so how you drive is up to you. Don't be nervous, any questions, just fire away. If I don't know the answer, someone back at the dealership will.'

'When was the last service carried out on the car?'

'The owners' service record should be in the glove box.' Let's see, twisting the catch, holding the glove box door so it doesn't hit my leg. Here it is, one service record book for the car, plus these bits of paper with details of other work carried out on the car. According to this, the last M.O.T was carried out two months ago, so there's ten months left. The car had a full service with the M.O.T.'

'Has there been any major work carried out on the car?'

'No, just tyres, bulbs, and an oil change. As you can see, there's only twenty nine thousand miles on the clock, not bad for one lady owner. What do you think of the drive, Richard?'

'Not bad, handles the road well, nippy little beast.'

'Is it the car for you?'

'It could be, it's only for the weekends really and going down the pub on those summer nights.'

'Hopefully there won't be as many cars on the road when you go out compared to what there is during the weekdays. London roads are getting over congested, or so the papers say.'

'I can quite understand that. I used to get a bus into the city to work, but now I go on the underground - it's usually quicker.'

'Myself, I have to drive miles to get home on the south circular. It takes an hour and a half to move about twelve miles. That's bad.'

'How long have you been with the garage, Chris?'

'Since yesterday. I enjoy meeting people. I saw an advert in a magazine, I replied to it, now I'm here. I was selling pints of beer before this, and now look, I'm serving you.' I wasn't going to tell him I sold double glazing windows before this.

'Yes I do like this. What extras do you get when you purchase a car from your dealership?'

'Extras?'

'Like breakdown cover, warranty, car mats, and road tax.'

'I'll find out for you what they offer when we get back to the showroom.'

'I do like this car.'

'1.4 Zetec, is inexpensive to run. I'm sure a tank of petrol is no more then twenty five pounds. Cheap on the road tax now the government has brought in a new ruling for small cars, insurance will be cheaper being a 1.4, it must be economical on petrol.'

'Myself, I drive a 1.25 Fiesta, 15 pounds a week is what it costs to fill up the tank. I have to travel quite a few miles each week so I prefer these smaller cars personally, but everybody's different, that's why you have other dealerships around touting for your business. That's why I sell cars to please. Richard, just along this road, we should be back at the garage. As we drive past these two public houses, I notice that there is a brewery nearby.'

'That's right, Wandsworth, one of the oldest in the country. You can smell the hops for miles when they're brewing. It's a strong odour - smells a bit like boiling cabbage.'

'That's the smell I smelt yesterday. Well I know one thing, I won't be drinking any of that shit then.'

'I hear they do good lager, though.'

'What, out of a bottle. Richard, if you do a left here up the slope, then park over to your left where there is a parking bay. I need to go for a slash, so if you want to look over the car, be my guest.'

'How are you getting on with Mr Clarke, Chris?' my manager enquired.

'I need a jimmy, boss, just letting him have a look over it by himself, back in a sec. Ah bliss, now I can deal better with this man. I needed that. Well Richard, it's a clean car as they say, no scratches, those tyres still like new.'

'What's the price, five and a half grand, is there any movement on that?'

'Let's go inside and I'll get you a coffee. How much are you offering?'

'Four to four and a half grand.'

'Somehow I don't think so, but let's find out. Do you have milk and sugar?'

'Two sugars and white, just like my women.'

Stupid twat, bet he hasn't even got a girlfriend. Typical vending machine, takes your money but is sold out of what you want. White one sugar, that will do, poxy machine gives you what you don't want. 'Sorry, Richard, only gave one sugar.'

'Doesn't matter, wet and warm, just like my women.' What's that, half-dead? Why is it always me who gets these fucking idiots wherever I go? Now this guy's just like Jo fucking ninety, big rimmed glasses, brushed back blonde hair and teenage acne, or does he still use the razor his mum bought for him all those years ago. It might even be a sweat rash from the fat bastard.

'There you are, Mr Clarke , right, where were we?'

'What do you do for cash?'

'Normally drop me trousers and shout, "take me, take me", but it's not my money and not my car. I'll have to work the other way to try to get you the price and make everyone happy. If I said five thousand, two hundred and fifty pounds, one year's AA cover plus one year's warranty, and a tank of fuel. Altogether that's worth an extra seven hundred quid. Do we have a deal?'

'Can I just think about it?'

'Chris, how are you doing with Mr Clarke?' my manager asked.

'He wants to think about it.'

'I told him five and half grand plus AA or green flag cover, one year's warranty worth an extra seven hundred.'

'I'll let him chat to his mother. He wants the car, give him five minutes.'

'OK, you've got a deal, Chris.'

'Nice one, Richard. Can I take a deposit from you?'

'How much would you like?'

'Five hundred pounds, please.'

'Credit card or cheque?'

'If you have a credit card, I'll take five hundred pounds off that.'

'Here you are. There should be sufficient funds in that one.'

'Let me write your order out. Now, when would you like the car?'

'Friday afternoon.'

'The reason why I ask, a cheque takes seven days to

clear so you won't get your car till the cheque clears. That will be next week. A bankers draft is like money. If you get one of those for the outstanding amount, you can take the car that day.'

'I'll get you a bankers draft.'

'That's fine. You need to bring with you, yourself and your insurance. We don't tax the cars because that's putting another name on the log book, dropping the value of the car. Mr Clarke, if you would like to read this contract, then sign if you're happy. It tells you what you're buying, the make and model, colour, engine size, the registration number for your insurance purposes, how much the car will cost, the deposit you've given, the VAT, and the last figure is what we require when you come to collect on the said day.'

'That looks okay to me.'

'If you would like to sign there, there, and there. Here you are, use my pen. Now I have to sign it there, just under your name. I'll date it. The amount of paperwork, I'm told, that's involved in selling a car is unbelievable. By the time you pick your car up, I'll have gone through about two trees. Here's your receipt for your credit card. One receipt is for what you have just signed for, and this item you have to sign for is to say if I have done a good job for this company by selling you this car. I thought they would be happy with the car going out of the forecourt - it's called company bullshit.'

'We all go through that. My company wanted us to wear our name tags every lunch time if we go to a pub over the road from where we work. So if someone got merry and started falling around on the floor, he'd get reported. The only trouble with that is, we all thought, "what a good company to work for. They're enjoying themselves, they must work for a relaxed company", so we went and joined them.'

'You must be bloody mad. Anyway, if there's any problems, just give me a call. Here's a business card with our phone number on. I'll put my name on so you won't forget it was me who sold you the car. See you Friday, at what time?'

'Between three and five. It all depends what time I get away from work. I'll give you a phone call to tell you I'm on my way.'

'That's fine, Richard, we will have the car ready and waiting. Safe journey home, thanks again, see you on Friday.'

That was it. I had sold my first car. It was easy. What a buzz! Now I understand why people get into the trade. Even my manager said, 'well done, Chris, put it up on the board.' The owner said, 'thanks', and shook my hand. OK, slow down, don't get carried away.

'Chris, can you phone your girlfriend. She called about half an hour ago and asked for you. I didn't know your name and told her we don't have a person by that name here, sorry.'

'That's all right, Terry. How did she find this number out so quickly? I suppose I'd better call her.'

'Hi love, guess what I sold, um so you're interested, okay.'

5

Losing the Plot Big Time

Not every deal is easy. We all like the couple or the single person entering the showroom without a part-exchange and the rigmarole of giving a price to suit when they bring a car with them. Some people want shed loads for their old shitters. Cars that your local salvage yard would expect you to pay them for to take them off your hands. These people must go round to every dealership with a figure in their head, expecting them to agree with the price that they require. Before they set out on a journey to find the right price wearing their rose-coloured glasses, or their mate that knows a lot about bugger all on cars. Those people must have a mental blockage in their heads. Whatever you tell them, it just passes over their heads.

All main dealers have a bible called the Glass's guide. This little book has every British car on the road, what value it is that said month, every car made in the last five to eight years. It shows how much a car value has dropped on a month-to-month basis. They all go by it.

Then there are the other idiots who come to the dealership with those reference books they have got from the newsagent. It happens all the time. 'You should give this price for my car, it says so in here, look.'

'But sir, the car must be top dollar, no dents, no scratches, and no rust. Look, your car has a bald tyre. Did you paint this masterpiece yourself? Look at the seats. Are your mates from the stone age? There's more hair on them than on my head, so your car's worth this price here.'

Then there are the drivers who have no idea what the car is worth.

'Well that's a choice V.W. car, sir. It drives like a brand new car for a three-year-old. Let me get you a part-exchange price on your car, won't keep you waiting long. Would you like a coffee?'

'Yes please, white with sugar, thanks.'

'How much are you looking for on your car?'

'I have no idea. Let's say the market value.'

To the sales manager's office I go, armed with my appraisal form.

'There you are, Jeff, all done. I've taken the car out for a spin, feels like a new car. It's up against a new Golf. What are you going to give for this?'

'Lets have a look, gun silver, that's what I call it, those miles are low, how much is he looking for?'

'The market value.'

'What car is it up against, a new V.W. Golf G.T T.D P.T, the 130 bhp in reflex silver is sixteen and a half grand on the road.'

'Let's give him nine and a half grand. It's worth ten plus, but we will try and nick it, as they say.'

'Mr Johnson, my sales manager, has offered nine and a half grand for your car at this stage. I advise you to sell your car privately, you'll get more money for it.'

'I don't want the hassle. OK, I'll take that price.'

'Right, let's work it out. The car's sixteen and a half, your part-ex is ten and a half, that leaves six thousand to pay.'

'Six grand, When do I get the car?'

'I think about three weeks, but I'll find out from my boss in a moment.'

'Six grand, three weeks. Throw some rubber mats in and you've got a deal.'

'One moment then, and I'll finalise the deal with my manager.'

This is going to be a good deal for the company. We've stolen this car, and I'm selling the new car with no discount - result!

'Hi boss, I think we have a good deal here. He's happy with the part-ex price that you offered, so how much is it going to make?'

'Let me see, that off the new, that for his old car, about three grand in that deal, not bad.'

'Anyway, he's happy with the colour. I told him the car will be here in three weeks. If he signs today, can we throw in some rubber mats? They're about twenty pounds.'

'If he wants rubber mats, he'll have to buy them himself.'

'Do what, we're going to make near on three grand

profit, and you won't spare a set of rubber mats? You're having a bubble bath.'

'Like I said, if he wants rubber bloody mats he buys them. Now fuck off and tell him.'

At this time of the deal, you don't want to lose it. You have to please both parties. Talking to the manager when he has a strop on, well you might as well bang your head against the wall.

'Mr Johnson, my manager said if you want some mats, you'll have to buy them yourself.'

'How much is a set of mats?'

'A set of rubber mats for your new car will set you back twenty pounds.'

'I guess that you've taken the piss out of me. I reckon you've taken fuck all off the new car, tucked me up on my part-exchange, and he won't throw in a set of rubber fucking car mats. Go and tell your manager he can go and do himself. I'll leave it and go somewhere else. Go tell him that.

'Ok, I guess you heard that, boss, he's going to walk.'

'Let him.'

'For the sake of twenty pounds, you're going to let him walk. What's your problem?'

'I have no problem, like I said, if Mr nice twat wants mats he can buy them himself. Where is the hardship in that? Now f'off out of here. This not an f'ing charity shop where we give things away. I'm here to make money.'

'You have lost the plot big time. For twenty quid, you are going to lose out here if he walks.'

'Let him.'

'Look, we're not talking about a compact disc player. All he asked for was a set of rubber car mats that are worth twenty quid.'

So back to the customer I go.

'Sorry, Mr Johnson my manager, who I can't believe, said if you want the mats you'll have to buy them yourself. The boss must be on drugs.'

'It's all right. I've been here what, two hours. I'm going.'

'I'll tell you what. I'll buy the rubber mats for you.'

'No, forget it, His loss. Sorry mate, I'm going.'

Off he went, never to return.

The next sales call I take was another wind-up.

'Hello, I am thinking of up-grading my car, so can you tell me the pulling power on your estate cars?'

Now what kind of question is that?

'I don't know the cars. My mate drives a V.W convertible, 206 convertible, I like those, then there's always the Audi, you can pull anything in that. What about the stretched limousine? Go to one of the clubs in town. I'm sure there'll be some there you could pull.'

'It's to pull a bloody caravan.' With that he put the phone down.

'Am I reading this right about the brand new Micra? You're giving two years free insurance, three years warranty, plus breakdown cover for two years as well.'

'That is right, as long as you're twenty one and over, 5995 on the road is the car for you.'

'No, for my young daughter. She drives an old clapped-out Vauxhall. Can she part-exchange it?'

'Sure, just tell her to bring it along. I'll make sure she get a fair price for the car.'

'If I gave you the details of the car, could you not give me a price over the phone.'

'Sorry, that would be unfair to your daughter. I might give you a price which undervalues the car, then again, I could say that the car is worth a lot more, and have trouble selling it on. We really need to see the car so we can inspect the vehicle. Tell you what, when she is free, just drive down to us. We will look after her, but if you're worried, come in with her. Do you live in the area?'

'Just on the outskirts of the town.'

'When is your daughter free to come to the showroom?'

'She finishes work at four this afternoon. What time do you close?'

'We all like to be away from here by six o'clock and go home to our loved ones.'

'I'll try and get her in later. When we have finished talking, I'll give her a phone call.'

'When you do come in, ask for me, my name's Barry. Your name is, sir?'

'Graham Bleaufield, I'll try and get her in some time this afternoon.'

'OK, Mr Bleaufield. I may see you later.'

They have tables to show what are the best selling cars per year, with Ford up the top, and down the bottom end of the table, Nissan, Skoda, Seat. There is nothing wrong with these cars, in fact Nissan is owned by a French company, while the latter two vehicle are owned by a German company. If Skoda got rid of that horrible green emblem on the front of their cars, people might take them seriously. They have lovely looking cars, then they put that on it, it spoils them.

'Is your customer driving a silver Corsa, Barry?'

'That must be Miss Bleaufield. Her dad said he would try and get her in. Look at the state of that heap of shit. She must be desperate to get out of that.'

Into the showroom walks a young girl, no more then five foot two, slim-built and quite attractive. She made her way to the receptionist, who in a polite way pointed towards my desk.

'Hello, I'm Sharon. My Dad phoned up earlier, and he said to come and see you.'

'That's right, my name's Barry. He said that you were after a new car, the Micra with the free insurance.'

'So, do you think you can give me a price on my car, please?'

'Are you requiring a new car today? Please don't be nervous. I don't bite. I'm here to help you choose a car.'

'Sorry, I've never been in a showroom like this before. We hear all those stories of what salesmen are like.'

'Well you are safe with me. I won't treat you badly. If you don't want a car, simply get up and leave. I thought your father was coming in.'

'He might be in later if I like a car. "Don't sign anything till he is here", he told me. I saw the advert in the local paper - the free insurance caught my eye.'

'Well, here is a brochure on the Micra. Would you prefer a three-door or a five-door?'

'I would like a three-door in dark blue.'

'A 1.0, a 1.2,or a 1.4?'

'A 1.4.'

'Let's have a look. The price for that car on the road, taxed for a year, will cost you £5995… oh and a full tank of petrol.'

'How much will you give me for my old car? It's a good little runner.'

'Sharon, what I'm going to do is take an appraisal of your car. It will tell me what the bodywork's like, how good the engine is, what the overall condition of your vehicle is like, so if I may take your car keys, I will go and look at your car. Have you had the car long, Sharon?'

'Three years, next month.'

'Lets see what we can offer on your car. It's on the D registration which tells me it's a 1987, which makes this car old. The car is worth nothing to us, £50. But let's go have a chat with my boss. Sharon, if you just grab a chair, back at my desk, I'll be two minutes. I'll see what he says.'

'Is it all right to have a look at these cars here?'

'Sure, feel free. When I come back, I'll take you out on a test drive. Then you can see what you think of the Nissan Micra.'

In the manager's office:

'It's a piece of shit. I told her it's worth fifty pounds. What do you think, Joe?'

'Barry, you old sperm whale, what is it up against?'

'One of those Micras, Joe.'

'I love you, Barry, when you get an old shitter in. Tell her that her lovely piece of crap is worth twenty-five pounds. No, I can't be that mean. We'll give her two hundred and fifty pounds. Give me that form. I'll sign to say the price is right. She will cream her knickers because we're taking that heap off her hands.'

'Cheers boss, I'll break the good news to her.'

Where did she go?

'I'm here, Barry.' Stepping out of a car.

'What do you think of this car? It has power steering, sun roof, that switch is for the electric windows. Let me take you on a test drive. I'll find a car that's similar so you can see what it drives like. It should take twenty minutes, is that all right?'

Outside, our forecourt was like a giant car park. So, hunting for a car takes a bit longer than anticipated, but I found it after a while.

'Right Sharon, this way to where the car's waiting.'

'Who's driving?'

'You can, just get yourself comfortable, the seat moves forward and backwards. The steering wheel moves up and down. That switch is for those mirrors. It's a lot different from the car you're driving at the moment. Turn right out of the forecourt, then head towards the motorway, off at the next junction down the dual carriageway, then we will be back here, just going in a large circle.'

'So what are you going to give me for my car?'

'How much are you after?'

'My Dad's friend said it's worth about four hundred pounds.'

'Why don't you sell it to him, or sell it privately. You will always get more money. We just give you the true value of your car.'

'So what are going to offer, Barry?'

'I'll tell you back at the garage. So how are you going to fund this car if you buy it?'

'I was going to get a bank loan, and Dad was lending me the other half.'

After engaging in idle chit chat we got back to the showroom. Then I had to tell her how much the company was going to give her for the part-exchange.

'Would you like a cup of tea, coffee, or a cold drink, or a nice cup of ice-cold water?'

'Iced water would be great, please.'

'Right, you car is worth to us, fifty quid, but with the discount we're going to give you, two hundred and fifty pounds.'

'Oh, I was hoping for three to four hundred.'

'If you sold your car privately, you might get an extra fifty to a hundred pounds. It's an old car. It's done a hundred and thirty thousand miles and it's got the odd rust patch coming through so it's not a car we would sell on. I mean, does your car have power steering, sun roof, rear wash and wiper?'

'No, but it still has an engine and an M.O.T.'

'So, as I say, sell it privately. You might get someone who's desperate for a car, knock on your door and pay you what you want, but I don't think so.'

'Well, Dad's friend said not to accept anything less than three hundred and fifty pounds, so that's what I was hoping for. Two hundred and fifty pounds - well, that's a hundred pounds less.'

'What does your father's friend do for a living, sell cars?'

'No, he's a London cabby.'

'So when he's driving around London and sees a car like yours up for sale by the side of the road, he thinks that's the price you should be asking for. Well it doesn't work like that. Each car is different. One car might have low mileage - that means a lot to a seller compared to a high mileage vehicle. The engine's big ends could go at anytime. It's a chance you take when buying a used car. What a lot of people do. They buy the local newspaper to see if there is a make or model of a car like the one they own, appearing anywhere, so they can get an idea what their car is worth and what they should be asking for it price wise. That's how it works. I've an old banger outside my house. I know that I'll get knocked down but I just want to get shot of it.'

'OK, I'll go along with what you are saying.'

'So you can either sell your car privately or part-exchange it. Like I said, it's not a car we want. My job is to get you into a new and reliable vehicle. So when you are whizzing around in your lovely new car, people will be wondering where you got that car from? So if you buy a car from any one of our dealerships, and anyone of your family or friends purchase a vehicle from one of our other dealerships as well, you get fifty pounds cash back. So, if ten of your friends that you know buy a car, you receive five hundred pounds. That's not bad, is it?'

'So you will give me three hundred pounds for my car?'

'Sharon, do you want this car, yes or no?'

'Yes.'

'Sharon, if I go and ask my manager, my boss, for any

more money, I'm going to get a size twelve boot up my backside, then have to tell you to go elsewhere, sorry.'

'It was worth a try. I'll go with what has been offered.'

'Right, let's do the paperwork.'

Then there was a phone call on her mobile. Guess what, it was her Dad telling her not to sign anything till he gets there. Ten minutes later, he's here and turns up in a black taxi. He's a cabbie. They're worse than salesmen ripping people off. She explains to her father what the deal involves and what I've told her. She ended up signing for the car about two hours later when everyone had gone home.

The dad, no disrespect to him, but he was thick as shit which is bad for a taxi driver. Explaining to two brainless dead persons that the car we were taking in was worth no more than a Saturday night out, can really harm you. Two hours of, "can't you give her three hundred pounds for her car", from her Dad. I don't know how many times I said no to the old man.

'Well, can she have car mats?'

'They come free with the car, it also comes with mud flaps, light protectors, CD player, air bags, front and rear fog lights, and rear spoiler. The Micra is a nice car and I would like to go home.' That's when she finally gave me a deposit. I made sure it was a large one, one thousand five hundred pounds. Then told her if she pulls out of the deal, she would forfeit her deposit. Out came the credit card. I could understand where she gets her knowledge. From her Dad, Mr light bulb.'

'The first service. Is she going to get that free?'

'No, that's going to cost her two hundred pounds, only

joking, that's free, courtesy of Nissan, so if I can have a signature here, pointing to the little box. Thank you, we will have your car ready for you next Friday. Can I have a signature here, pointing to another box. That's for the free insurance.'

'Can't you make the car any cheaper before she signs?'

I just looked at him and let what he said go over my head while putting all the paper together in a file. 'If I reduce the car any more, you might as well come back tomorrow and buy a used car. You will lose out on the free insurance and whatever a new car has to offer. Thank you, Sharon, I know you will be happy with the car you're going to get, so see you next Friday about four o'clock. Please bring with you a building society cheque. Please don't bring your Dad - he has lost the plot.'

I took my wife to London's West End for a day and night. We went to the pictures, then had a meal in Covent Garden. We needed to get a cab to Victoria station to get the train home. We jumped into a black cab driven by the right honourable Mr Dick Head. We got the journey for free which was nice of him.

I was told to come back in a year's time. He might have something else to tell me.

6

What Do You Want For Breakfast - a No. 49?

'Phillip, answer the phone, it's been ringing for ages,' the manager shouted.

'Good morning, my name's Phillip. Thank you for calling this wonderful showroom, so how can I help you?'

'I callin abat kar, new kar that's in todas papar col foecus, yes.'

'Excuse me madam, but are you're calling about the Ford Ka?'

'Yer new kar for foecus I see in papar in mornin yes u got kar ther in showroom.'

'Please mam, what's your name?'

'Me Wong tha Mis Wong.'

'Mrs Wong, I just want to put you on hold.'

'Yer, OK.'

'Oh no, I've hit the jackpot here - a lovely lady from the far east who speaks broken English. Sorry, I can't stop laughing every time she says a word. I just can't help it.

Can anyone speak the tongue of China, cos this lady is going to be hard work, ah john sucky sucky.'

Back on the phone: 'Sorry to keep you waiting Mrs Wong. You phoned regarding the new Ford Focus, the one in our showroom.'

'Yes, I see you cell kar I come down to see kar, tak kar for dive.'

'Mrs Wong, you want to come to the showroom, then take a Focus out for a test drive.'

'I come dow vun tirty, I be dare.'

'So you're coming in at one thirty to test drive the car. Do you have a full driving licence?'

'I hav a licence OK.'

'Mrs Wong, you know where our showroom is?'

'No wurrwe I get taxcy, he bring me to see you.'

'Well, we're just off the upper Richmond road. You can't miss us. We have all the flags hanging on the railings. Look forward to seeing you, you understand?'

'No I understand taxcy find you.'

'Well, see you at 1.30. Goodbye.'

'Bye.'

Ho sugar, we have got a Chinese woman coming here for a test drive on a car. This is going to be hard work with the communication barrier. That is, I don't speak her lingo, and she isn't going to understand a word I'm saying.

'Go on Phil, sell her a car. You like a challenge,' came a shout from one of the other salesmen.

Sure enough, 1.30, on to the forecourt drives the taxi carrying Mrs Wong. She looked like a small schoolgirl, then out of the car she steps, no taller then five foot.

Get this picture, if you ever see a horse racing jockey being interviewed by a reporter on the television. How tall are they - 5 foot to 5 feet 6? Then you have someone the size of your front door, most doors are about 6 foot 6 inches to 7 foot high. It was quite funny watching this lady making her way to the reception. With her head bobbing up and down between the cars, she looked like the cleaner washing the cars. She arrived at the reception area and could just see over the counter.

'I come to see Phil,' she said to our receptionist. Then, in her polite receptionist manner, she called out for the salesman.

'Phil to reception, make it snappy, Phil to reception,' came the voice over the loud speaker.

Now Phillip is not small - well over 6 foot tall (remember the size of the door), built like a brick shit house, one of those men who has a very placid, laid-back manner until someone ruffles his feathers. I remember he was going out on a test drive when this guy was filling his car with petrol and blocking the way through to get off the forecourt.

'Excuse me, sir, do you think you can just move your car forward so I can squeeze past?'

'In a minute. Can't you see I'm filling up?' came the reply.

'But I need to get out to get on this test drive.'

'You'll just have to wait, won't you?'

'Look, I have asked you nicely, so hurry up. I have these people in the car and we want to get going, or I lose the deal.'

'Like I said, you'll just have to wait.'

Big mistake. He walked up to the guy and knocked him out with one swift blow. Then he moved the man and the car and went out on his test drive.

'This is Mrs Wong, Phillip,' the receptionist said with a huge smile on her face. 'Phillip, your customer awaits you.' That smile from the receptionist summed up what we all felt.

'This way, please, Mrs Wong,' he said, showing the lady towards his desk. 'Thank you Miss receptionist, I'll remember this.'

'Wer kar Phillip? I like to see kar.'

'If I can take a photocopy of your driving licence for insurance purposes only, it will only take a moment.' She has a European one at that, but it was full. How did she get this?

After a couple of minutes, the appraisal form was filled in, and up stood Mrs Wong.

'We go now Philwhip. I bring cushan I sit on in kar. I dive wer kar.'

'The car is parked just over there by the fence. It's the dark blue one, so follow me.'

Now, a test drive should take about twenty minutes, so the customer can get a feel of the car and see how it moves, steering, gears, what extras there are on a new car. Some salesmen like to go out a little longer. It all depends on what time of the day it is. It also keeps them out of the building.

'Here we are, this is a Ford Focus. Would you like me to drive, Mrs Wong, to see how it handles the road?' he offered.

Have you ever been in a situation, where you just want to burst out and cry with laughter, and you know you can't? Well, the whole sales team, even the managers, lined up to see them off. One guy offered Phil a crash helmet as they walked past towards the car.

'No, I dive, you tel wera we go. I know the woads wond here.'

So in the car they both get. Mrs Wong adjusts her cushion, then she starts the engine. By this time, everyone in the dealership was watching the events taking place. The place had a buzz of excitement in the air. Then the pair set off on the drive. The expression on the passenger's face was one of horror. The look you see on the faces of the people on a roller coaster ride as it's taking the plunge down that mega drop. The look of, 'oh shit, what have I done this for?'

With miss tweedy pie driving, who could only just see over the steering wheel, a horror movie was unfolding here. We could just make out the head of the driver - it was the small head of Mrs Wong. While they were setting off, we were creasing up with laughter. Now in most cars nowadays, you can adjust the seat to the position that you would feel most comfortable in, so if you are tall, you lower the seat with a lever that's on the bottom part under the chair. The same is required to make the seating position higher. Letting someone drive who could hardly see over the dashboard was not very professional, was it?

Normality returned to the workplace five minutes after they had gone. Most hadn't had so much to laugh at for years, and were seen wiping away the tears.

Time went by, and after an hour and a half they return. She parks the car in the bay provided, and both get out. Phillip takes the keys, shakes her hand, and the lady walks off. He locks the car up, walks out of the forecourt and into the pub next door where he orders two large brandies to calm his nerves.

'You all right, mate?' our manager asked, as he followed him into the pub.

Taking a big gulp of his drink, he said, 'I've been on hundreds of test drives in my time as a salesman, some funny, some not, been out with boy racers, slow coaches, been driven by real drivers, some who knew what they were doing, some who didn't. I told her this has been Ford's best car for years. The best car ever to hit the car market for a while now. Other car manufactures will have to copy, and will have to play catch-up. This car will lead for years. At the moment, this is the best family car on the road.'

'Go on,' he said.

'Did you see that she even brought her own cushion in. She could just about see over the dashboard (still shaking while telling his plight to our boss). I don't know how many cars we only just missed. The number of times we stopped from going up the arse of the car in front. I'll never know how she managed to stop when she did. She was standing up every time she applied the brakes. It was worse then banger racing, but without hitting another car. She didn't even want the car. She was sitting at the breakfast table with her son when he mentioned about test driving a Focus because one of his mates had just got one as a company car. That's all, just talking. He was going to test

55

drive one this weekend, so she wanted to beat him to it. They didn't want a new car. They each have a new car at home. She said if I go to their takeaway food place, she will make up for wasting my time. She was a kamikaze driver - never again!'

He was still shaking when he left to go home that evening, but then it could have been the drink.

'Hello, I'm phoning to ask if you sell cars?'

'Yes we do, can I help?'

'Do you sell blue cars?'

'Blue, red, white, and green.'

'I only wanted to know if you sold blue cars. I wasn't asking if you had any other colours. If I wanted a red, green, black, orange, or silver, I would have asked, wouldn't I?'

'Mr...'

'Yes, what?'

'Piss off.'

Down went my phone.

7

Taken for a Ride, Me? Never

'Good morning, I'm interested in a test drive of your leading car, today if possible.'

'Sure, can I just get my diary? What's the name, please?'

'Peter Williams.'

'Mr Williams, what sort of time were you thinking of, and what model of the Ford range were you wanting to drive?'

'About 2.30, and I would like to test drive the 2.0 litre three-door Zetec Ford Focus.'

'Yes, that's fine, do you know where our showroom is?'

'Yes I do, but I was hoping you would meet me from my place of work.'

'Where is that, where do you work?'

'Next to Brixton train station. It's the record shop next door. I was hoping you could pull up and give me a quick call on my mobile. I'll come out and jump into the car. Is that all right?'

'There's all those traffic wardens around there at that time of the day, so if I get a ticket I'll give it to you.'

'You won't get a ticket. They'll be gone by the time you get here. Look, take my phone number, and I'll give you my mobile number too.'

'Sure, fire away.'

Strange that those two numbers are different from the one that's showing on my screen, and he's phoning on a mobile. I might as well take this one, and have three. I know most salesmen like to leave the showroom once in a while, so as long as this is a genuine test drive I don't mind going out, but I have a sneaky suspicion that this bloke is going to use me as a taxi ride.

Brixton train station. Which way do I go to get there? Should I go over Clapham Common or past Clapham junction train station? No, I'll go over the Common, Clapham Park Road into Acre Lane, left into Brixton Road, and there should be the station. It took twenty minutes to get there. At 2.30, I'm outside the shop. I'll park up and give him a call on his mobile, so let's turn the car around and just wait. Where's my phone - his phone number is on this piece of paper, key in the number, push the button, there. I get, 'The number you are trying to reach is switched off, please try later'. You what! I'll try this other number, his shop, a young lady answers the phone.

'Is Peter there, please?'

'I'm afraid he's not.'

'Do you know what time he will be back?'

'No, I don't.'

'Don't worry, I'll call him on his mobile.'

So I decided to call on the third number I had - this number rang.

'Hello.'

'Peter, isn't it?'

'That right, who's that?'

'Your test drive, the one you booked up earlier.'

'Oh shit, sorry mate, I completely forgot, it slipped my mind. I'll have to give it a miss. Can I make it tomorrow? I'll tell you what, I'll come to the dealership. I know where it is, say 8.30?'

'Yeah, whatever. If you say so.'

'I got caught up in something outside of work, but I will be there for eight thirty.' We don't start work until nine so that means an early start from home for me. 'I know where the showroom is,' he continued, 'so I will see you in the morning.'

Why do I get the feeling that this dick head is taking the piss out of me? He seemed a decent bloke over the phone. I should listen to my elders - let the customer run after you. It looks that way here, I'm running after him. Eight thirty, no show, eight forty-five he turns up.

'You must be Peter Williams. My name is Paul. Thanks for turning up.'

'Where is the car, Paul?'

'Before we go, do you have your driving licence on you? I need to take a photocopy.'

'Yes I have. It's the old-fashioned type, no mug shot.'

'That's all right, it's only for insurance purpose. While I'm doing this, would you like a coffee?'

'No thanks.'

'Right, this way Mr Williams. I have the keys, here's your driving licence. Here is the Ford Focus, two litre petrol, three-door zetec with all mod cons such as ABS, ESP, PAS, air con, driver's airbag, passenger's airbag, side airbags, room for the shopping bags, multi-change CD player, radio with cassette, remote central locking, satellite navigation. This one also has leather sports seats. She's a lovely car - the only snag is that it's the rush hour and you'll not get the complete benefit out of the car.'

'Can I take it to Trinity Road, just to get a feel? There's no speed cameras there.'

'Any speeding tickets, I send them straight to you.'

Trinity Road is a dual carriageway, no more than a couple of miles long. If you're quick, you can reach a hundred plus but we don't encourage it. So off we set, taking it nice and easy.

'Enjoy the car, you can feel that she wants to go.'

Driving away from the traffic is something I'm not used to this time of the morning. Along the A214, reaching a speed of a hundred and forty, then hitting the brakes. Left into Balham High Road over Clapham Common, right into Clapham Park Road, funny, I came this way yesterday and have a sneaky feeling this guy is taking me to his work place. A test drive should take about forty-five minutes. We arrive outside his shop an hour after setting off.

'Cheers mate, nice car, driving it gives me something to chew on through the day. I don't think I'll be getting one of these though.'

'Saved you the bus fare, didn't it?' I said, as I jumped out of the car and into the driver's seat. Here I am stuck in the sodding bus lane, what a pratt. Adjusting the seat to suit me, I find a mobile phone at the side. Well it's not mine, I wonder whose it could be, so I gave my sister a call - she lives in Australia - then I gave my friend a call while he's in America. You don't take me for a ride.

Later, back at the showroom.

'There's been a call for you. The guy you went out on a test drive with this morning thinks he's left his mobile in the car.'

'Shame, if he wants me to be his personal driver, I'm going to need a phone.'

8

The Time Waster

'Who wants to take this call?' The words we love to hear from the receptionist.

'Put it through, I'll take it. Martin speaking, how can I help?'

'The name's Bower, Stuart Bower. I see Ford have brought out a new car. Well, I'm calling because I can't get to you so, this might sound a bit of a cheek but do you think there's a remote chance that you can bring the car to me so I can take it for a test drive?'

'Do live far from here, Mr Bower?'

'Just off the common.'

'What sort of time were you thinking of?'

'About four thirty this afternoon.'

'It's one thirty now, so that shouldn't be a problem. Can I take a contact number please, oh and the address?'

Martin spends the best part of two hours getting the car ready, taking it out of the showroom, putting enough petrol in for the test drive. He checks the local map of the area to find out exactly where he has to go, then leaves just before four o'clock. It's going to be busy on the roads this time of day, people going home from work, the schools run and Wimbledon Common. No, he wasn't going to burst into song - he couldn't stand the Womble song when it came out - so up goes the radio volume to drown out those faults. Bramble Close, that must be around here according to this map, number 309 must be this house here. That's handy, parking space right outside the house. With the car parked up, Martin gets out of the car to meet the client, Mr Bower. Nice house he thinks, walking up the path. He presses the door bell and waits, and waits, then a gentleman answers the door.

'Hello, my name is Martin from Browns Ford. I'm here for the test drive with a Stuart Bower. I hope I'm not too early - we did say four thirty.'

'Well, that's me, but I never booked a test drive with you.'

'You what, I had a conversation with a Mr Bower this afternoon, and he gave me this address and phone number.'

'Hold on son, I've been at work all day, and got home five minutes ago. As you can see, this is my car,' he said, pointing to a Mercedes. 'This is my company car, the other car there is my wife's car.' Pointing at a V.W Golf. 'So you can see, I don't need another car. Wait here a moment.'

He goes back into the house which is in the quieter area of Wimbledon, a tree-lined avenue. Most of the properties must be worth, three-quarters of a million. Waiting on the doorstep in this quiet residential area, the air turns blue. Shouting - I've never heard anything like it. This man must have a military background, he's just like a sergeant major shouting out marching orders over the parade ground. Martin thought he could swear, but the words he heard that day he would use on us all week. Twenty minutes later, Mr Bower came back out of the house.

'That bloody boy, lazy little shit.'

'What's he done?'

'Every time a new car comes on the market, he's on the phone to the nearest dealership asking to test drive the car. You're not the first salesman to show up on my doorstep with a new car. He's not even old enough to drive, he's only sixteen. Sorry for wasting your time, Martin,' he said, pulling out his wallet. 'Here you are,' as he handed a twenty pound note over to me. 'That's for the trouble he's caused.'

'Next time he's interested in a car, get him to ring the dealership and ask for a brochure.'

Back at the showroom. 'How did you get on today, Martin?' the boss asked.

'The little shit was only sixteen, doesn't even have a fishing licence let alone a driving licence. He just wanted to look the new car over, does it all the time apparently, what a bloody waste of time. I'm going home now, see you tomorrow.' The phone rings...

'Do you have any beetles in stock?'

'No, Rentokill have terminated them, now we're bug-free.'

9

Well It Surprised Me Too!

'Good morning, Mrs Davidson, it's Gary from the S.M garage. I know it's early - just gone nine - so I thought I would phone you to see if you're at home. You came into our showroom last Saturday with your husband, I believe, looking for a small car for your daughter?'

'Good morning to you, Gary (I love the accent of the South African ladies' voices). Thit's right, an automatic car. We didn't mind if it was a Fiesta or Corsa, any small car. You were going to hunt and scour the country. So what have you found?'

'One of our underwriters has been searching on my behalf and found a Fiesta that this lady is willing to sell to us. I just need to know if you require that car?'

'Please tell me more about this car. What's the colour, how many doors, where have you found it, the price is how much? It's very exciting.'

'As I was saying, one of our company underwriters

remembers me asking if they could find a car. I gave them all the details that they wanted. Well I just had a phone call, one of them is in the Southampton area today buying some cars. Well, they have found one for you. It's a Ford Fiesta, three doors, in metallic burgundy red. The car is only two and a half years old. He also informs me that there are only twenty thousand miles on the clock which is low for that aged car - £4750.00. We have a driver standing by to go down and pick the car up if you want it.'

'Thit sounds like the car we want. What I'll do, if you can stay on this line, I'll phone Richard and see what he wants to do.'

In the background, I could hear the talking going on with her high pitch voice.

'Hello Gary, my husband said yes, so how much do we need to give you?'

'The price of the car is £4750.00, but before we let you have the vehicle we have to give it a full safety check, oil, lights, then a full valet to make the car look like new. So you can either pay a holding deposit or the full amount?'

'We will pay in full so I might as well give you the credit card number over the phone.'

'Sure, fire away.'

'It's 4920…'

I knew she was going to buy this car. The driver we have on standby was an old gas meter reader man. He joined the company three weeks ago as a driver, now he's a car jockey who is sent out to either pick up or deliver a car. He's been with S.M Motor for three weeks but he's not one you would trust with your eggs, so to

Southampton he was going to be sent. What a thicko.

'Thank you, Mrs Davidson. I'll send you copies of the order and your credit card receipt today, so you should get them in the next day or two. The car will take two days so, today being Thursday, say Saturday for you to pick the car up. If there's any problems, myself or someone else will call you. Once we get the vehicle, we need to check the oil, brakes, etc. We give it a safety check for peace of mind - that's what takes two days.'

'That's fine, it's little Sam's birthday on Saturday. I call her little but she's eighteen and it's also graduation day so it will be a nice surprise present for her. We will be in touch, thank you, Gary.'

She's in for a shock, a big shock.

'The train to Southampton leaves Waterloo at 10.35. I've phoned their booking office so we can get Dennis on his way now, if we can.'

'OK, I'll phone James, the buyer. He will give me the address for the pick-up, so give me a few minutes. Hello James, Peter here. That red auto - where does the lady live? We want to send the driver off ASAP, also did you get her phone number?' The manager carried on talking down the phone.

'The lady lives at a place called Thornhill, on the outskirts of Southampton. James is going to meet you at Southampton train station. This is his car reg, and the car he's driving is a silver 406. He'll be waiting for the driver.'

'Dennis, get the man to the sales office now,' called the manager.

As I was saying, Dennis is an ex-Gasman, no more then

five and a half foot, very skinny with hair begging to be cut and washed. He's used to plodding around going from house to house, door to door in his own time. So when they asked him to go and get the car, my first reactions were that he was going to get lost on the train, go straight to a pub, get pissed for the day, and never come back. I just didn't trust him. A good job he wasn't taking the money with him or we would never seen him again. So, packed with mobile phone, a map of how to get on to the motorway, and train fare, Dennis was sent on his way.

The journey to the south coast should take forty minutes to an hour plus. It's quick to get there nowadays, so it should only take two to two and a half hours to get there and back - that's going on the M3 - it's a straight run back to south east London. So while that's going on, I'll get on with the paperwork - no hold-ups on my part, tea-break time and a quick cigarette.

A couple of hours later. 'Hello Dennis, have you picked up that car yet?'

'Yes, and it's such a lovely day down here, I decided to take the scenic route back, me and this little car are just going past Petersfield on the A3. For an automatic, this car is a good runner. I'm not thrashing it, just sticking at a steady speed. She's moving like a new car.'

'Any old pile of shit is a new car compared to what you drive, Dennis. You're going to be hours, just don't wreck the car.'

This is how a salesman earns his money. Once a car leaves the forecourt, all the work has been done, money has been paid so there's nothing outstanding on the vehicle.

The file goes to the wages office. They work out what the profit is on the car and take your percentage off. If you have six to seven cars a week leaving the site, it all mounts up to quite a bit of money. The more you have going out, the better the wages. You really don't want any hiccups, so when someone has two other cars going out that afternoon, there's a certain feel-good feeling going around.

It's a nice hot day, smiles on people's faces. The buying feeling is about couples walking on the forecourt, viewing cars, some buying, other salesmen on test drives. Moving cars that have been sold, parking them in the bay provided, the manager even mentioned, 'It looks like the weekend has started today so I'm treating the sales team to beers tonight.'

We know motorway driving can be boring. That's why they put service areas every sixty to hundred miles just to kill the monotonous time you're on your journey travelling. Don't they rip you off? Taking the A road now and again breaks up the boredom, so we couldn't really blame the driver taking an alternative route. The A3 from Portsmouth on the south coast passes through the south downs, Petersfield, then towards Guildford through Cobham, Chessington World of Adventure, buzzing in the summer when the schools are on holiday. Getting closer to London is when you pass Kingston upon Thames. This is where the speed camaras love to take your photograph. There's ways round it - ask any farmer in Norfolk who gets a speeding ticket - say no more on that subject.

So Mr Gasman arrives with the car six hours after setting out that morning which wasn't bad going. I know that getting a parking space on our forecourt is something of a rarity. With all the cars that got sold today, jostling for space, there's a lot of activity going on. When he turned up, he just had to be a bit patient, a space will appear once they have sorted the car forecourt. Now this car has just come from the south coast, not a scratch on the car, the alloy wheels setting the car off, colour coded bumpers, a nice runabout. All he had to do was put the handbrake on. That's all he had to do. He put the car in 'park', which stops the car moving forward. He got out of his car to see where he could park up, only for the owner to shout at him to, 'Move that fucking car now.' I suppose it was a shock to be spoken to like that.

'Can't you see we're moving the bloody forecourt about?'

With that he jumped back into the car and, instead of putting his foot on the brake, he had his foot on the accelerator, so when he changed gear and put it in reverse, it was like the start of a Grand Prix just waiting for the green light to show. No, he cheated, he jumped the lights. Bang, he hit a parked car, smashing the lights on both the one he was driving and the parked car.

Putting the gear into forward, smashing into two parked cars that were going out later that day, damaging both wings on the Fiesta, the lights, indicators, doors, all smashed, damaging four cars in the process of going backwards then forward. Talk about jumping the gun, he was the bullet. The two cars that were meant to be going out that afternoon didn't, and the Fiesta needed two weeks work done on it.

The owner of the car site calmly walked over to Den the gasman. By this time everybody was staring at what had just happened.

'May I have those keys please?'

'Sure.'

'Now go and get your personal belongings, please,' he said in a polite way of asking. Then with one almighty bellow instructed the stunned driver too, 'FUCK OFF and don't ever show your face here again.'

If the owner had had a shotgun close by, I swear I could have shot the man. So what do you tell those customers who are about to pick their cars up? Nothing, you let the manager tell them. That's what he's paid for.

10

Two Years Too Late

'Hello there. I was just browsing the local paper, hoping to find a small car, then came across your advert. It reads that you're well stocked up with small cars.'

'That's right, sir, Fiestas, Corsas, 106s, 206s, Fiats, Hondas, Rovers, Polos, even a Micra, so how small do you want the car to be?'

'I was wondering what was the cheapest car to run, such as insurance, road tax, petrol, the general maintenance costs per year. Would you be able to help me find a car to fill my needs?'

'Sure, what's your name please, so I know whom I'm talking to.'

'Robert Martell, Bob if you like.'

'Thanks Robert, my name's David. Say, when are you looking to get a car?'

'What about today, if you're not too busy? My girl-friend and I could come in, say, one to one-thirty, perhaps you could take us out on a test drive if we choose and like a car?'

'Certainly, just bring your driving licence. Robert, do you have a phone number I can reach you on just in case I have to do something else, or get called out of the office?'

'Sure, it will be a mobile.'

'That's fine, fire way.'

'077... Is that all right?'

'Great, if you hear from me, it's to change the time, if you don't, see you at 1 to 1-30. You know where we are and how to get here?'

'I know how to get there. I normally pass your showroom on the bus.'

'Thanks, Robert, see you then.'

This is going to be an easy deal, I hope, but knowing my luck! We will see. The last easy deal - the car was a boomerang - it kept coming back and coming back for weeks.

So, twenty past one they arrived. Time to go and introduce myself.

'Good afternoon, my name's David. You must be Mr Martell.'

'Afternoon David, I see you have plenty of cars here and so many to choose from.'

'Over here we have all the small cars from 900cc to 1400cc, pretty coloured ones, so some will take your fancy if you have a colour in mind. Go and see if there's a car that suits you.'

'Silver or dark blue are the colours we have in mind.'

'What I'll do is let you walk amongst the cars, then

when you find a car you like, come and get me. I'll get the keys and we'll take that car for a drive, is that all right?'

'Sure, where do we start?'

Twenty minutes later, my customers enter the showroom. I thought they had gone home.

'I think we've found one we like. It's the silvery blue 106. Can we have a look inside and see what the seating positions are like, and how much room there is?'

'I'll just get the keys for you.'

While they are having a rummage over the car, a few of my colleagues help move the cars that were in the front row. I get it out for a test drive. Ten minutes and we're ready for the off.

'That's not a bad price for this car. Was this in your price range? That's if you had a price in mind?'

'I hadn't thought of a price. I just wanted to buy a car if I liked it.'

I could make a killing here. I could put an extra grand on this car. Then flog it for the list price and I could pocket the difference, what a pratt. I should have asked that question on the phone before they got here, ah well, that won't happen again.

'Just move it toward the exit, who's driving?'

'I will, my girlfriend wants to stay here.'

'That's all right, if she would like to wait at my desk. We won't be long, miss.'

'These Peugeot 106 cars are one of the best small cars on the road. If it's just you and your girlfriend using it, then it's ideal, three doors, sun roof, I like this colour as well. Robert, get yourself comfortable, indicators are to your left hand side, lights, not that we need them, are to your right. I'm not a driving instructor so shall we begin. Been driving long, Robert?'

'On and off about two and a half years.'

'The route we're going to go will take us around the block. The drive shouldn't take us long, so if you drive towards the town centre we'll come upon a bridge. If you turn left there, follow the road to the top of the hill where you turn left again.'

'I'll try not to stall it.'

'Don't be nervous. Enjoy the drive.'

So off we set, heading towards the bridge, not much traffic on this road so it should be an enjoyable ride, service book in the glove compartment, and other bits of history.

'Is this the turning?'

'Next one.'

'OK.'

'What do you think of the car and the drive, Robert?'

'The car feels very good, the steering is light and easy to handle, feels roomy.'

'This is the turning, so slow down a bit. Don't run that old girl over, the one crossing the road now.'

He manages to manoeuvre that without any hitch, but I was beginning to wonder about his driving ability. You know when someone has confidence, they'll whizz around like a boy racer driving someone else's car. They drive to see how it handles the road, if the brakes are as sharp as theirs, gear changes, test the clutch. Well, his driving seemed strange. He gripped the steering wheel for dear life, and we were only going 20 miles an hour.

'Right, Robert, the road we're coming to is the south circular, one of the busiest roads in the south east, so when you see a gap, take it.'

'OK.'

It was like the start of a Grand Prix, engine revving, foot on the gas, clutch biting, then...

'FUCK ME, FUCKIN' HELL, WHAT THE FUCK have you done? You've pulled out from a junction onto one of the worst roads in London. Did you not see that car? Because I FUCKING did. I said look for a gap, meaning three cars distant, not a couple of feet. Pull over and let's have a look at the damage to both cars. Oh shit, one fucked offside wing, the door. Stay here, Bob, I'll go and see if that guy's all right.'

'What can I say, are you OK mate? Damaged front nearside window, front grill, lights – oh shit, sorry about that, you can still drive the car, mate.'

'I thought you were meant to stop at these junctions. It does say stop, look there's a sign, I wonder what it says.'

'Look, if you're not too busy, this is our garage,' I said, giving him one of my business cards. 'If you go there now, I'm sure they'll sort this problem out.'

'Where is your garage?'

'If you go down the road, turn right, and it's about a mile. You can't miss it. I'll be there in a couple of minutes.'

'Are you OK, Robert, not shaking are you?'

'I'm fine. What do we do now?'

'Drive back on the same route. They'll sort the car out, so don't worry. I thought you said that you've been driving for two years.'

'That's right, on and off, but I only passed my driving test on Tuesday...

'You FUCKING WHAT! THAT'S FUCKING TWO DAYS AGO. I knew there was something strange about your driving. You were on edge all the time you were driving, so you're still a learner. Oh shit, what the hell do I tell them back at the showroom. I'm going to be the laughing stock.

We got back to the showroom and parked up. The body shop estimated the damage to be twelve hundred quid. After the laughing and shouting had stopped, Robert sat down and signed, putting pen to paper for the smashed car.

He took delivery two weeks later. A packet of twenty cigarettes never calmed my nerves, but a stiff brandy...

Now when anybody phones for a test drive, I ask how long they have had their driving licence for, and what method of payment they are going to use.

11

The Mystery in Shopping

I remember a dealership in the south east of London I worked for. One site closed down and they had to transfer all inventory from one site to the other, files, computers, desks, cars, mechanics, drivers, and the office staff. They all moved to the other site about seven miles away. Those extra miles meant leaving home earlier in the morning, but it's all part of the job.

A new environment. We might make a few extra car sales. Eight extra salesmen - they might double the monthly car sales, but that never worked. Four used car salesmen and three new car salesmen left, and two sales managers as well.

When I worked for a large dealership, they often got paranoid. When it came to advertising, they'd go over the top - a full spread in the local weekly newspaper - must have cost a few bob. So by the end of the week we are swamped with phone calls asking about cars that we have on the forecourt. The job was to get them in. Once they were in, they would buy, or so we were told. When they did come in to the showroom to purchase a car, it was always the deposit they wanted to pay with someone else's credit card. What made us laugh was that not everyone who came into the showroom was refused credit. I would say 70% were. It wasn't just our dealership, those around a five mile radius of Greenwich had these wonderful people going around trying to buy cars with someone else's credit cards. The dealer principal of the site wanted us to prospect ten new people a day so we could get them in to buy a car. Prospecting is another way of advertising, cold calling, trying to build up trade by chasing people into buying a car, which never worked, but if you didn't like it, we were told to clear off. You soon get peed off getting people in that you sent home that week. The best one was going through the dead people's files, so then the management checked up on the phone calls you've made.

Then there's the other way to see if your sales team are doing their job right. We have the incoming calls four times a week. The people turning up just to make sure we're doing our job right.

The Saturday, the weekend before we moved, 'That's the car for you Mr and Mrs Dawson, I've been keeping people off this car all week, so do you want to take it for another drive before you make your mind up.'

'No, we're happy. We want to put a deposit down now, then pay the rest off during the week.'

'That's no problem, just give me a deposit so I can hold the car for you.'

'I'll give you five hundred pounds now, cash or card.'

'Whatever suits you.'

'Julie, can I have one of my cards, love, please?' the man asked his wife.

'Hold on,' she said, rummaging through her handbag. 'It's not in here, Richard, you must have left them at home.'

'I'll tell you what I'll do. You stay here, love, and I'll nip home. Should be about half an hour, is that all right with you, Nick?'

'Sure, Mrs Dawson, while your husband is going home, would you like a coffee?'

'Yes please.'

While my customer was sitting there, I spied a couple walking about between the cars. I asked the lady, while her husband wasn't here, if she minded that I went to ask what they wanted and come back when her other half returned? She said that was fine, so off I went.

'Good morning, I see you're looking at this. Are you looking at buying a car?'

'We might be. Could you get the keys so we can have a look and sit inside?'

'Give me a couple of minutes,' I said, going to the manager's office to get the keys. On the way back I noticed a camera lens poking through the lady's bag pointing at me. Why, the sneaky pair were mystery shoppers. I'm going to have a laugh with these two. Come down on a Saturday to catch us out, I'll show them.

'Hello, here's the keys. Have yourself a sit in the car. Every now and then I would burst into song which raised some eyebrows. Is it an automatic you want?'

'No, this isn't an auto.'

'So you want a 1.8 cc.'

'We were hoping for a small size engine. Is this a 1.8?'

'No, just asking what size engine you wanted.'

'Can you tell us a bit about the car?'

'As you can see, it has five doors, four wheels, it has 17000 thousand miles on the clock, one owner. Again, this car is also classed as a popular taxi driver's car amongst the mums who drive it on the school run. (Thinking of school, you can always spot a teacher by the way they dress in outdated old fashion, and they always look down their nose at you). As you can see, it has five doors, air conditioning, power steering, electric windows, and mirrors.

'What is the history on this car?'

'Well, the father is the engine, mother being the body, grandfather won the Grand Prix a few years back. This car has had a full service. The service book is in the glove compartment if you would like read it, in there.'

'No, it's a nice car.'

'So, do you want it?'

'We don't know. I see you have some small cars on the front of the forecourt. Can we go and see them?'

'How much are you budgeting on your next car? Do you have any idea what you want to spend?'

'When we find the right car, that is when we talk finance.'

Walking between the cars, I notice my customer has returned and is parking his old banger in one of the bays. I have been with this couple now for forty minutes, and no closer to getting a positive answer, so time to give them the elbow.

'Mr Dawson, I'll be with you in a couple of minutes.'

'Sure.'

'You have not finished with us yet, and we want to see the cars on the front of this forecourt.'

'You must think everyone you meet is stupid. You have no intention of buying a car today, tomorrow, or anytime this year. I noticed when you first came in to the showroom, the video camera lens poking out of your bag filming me. I have no intention of being in your next movie. I'm here to sell cars to people who want them. With you, I would have spent two to three hours of getting nowhere, and in that time I could have sold two or three cars. The people I was dealing with before you, want to purchase a car. They want to give me some cash to say they're committed to buying a car. So I'm not going to lose them. What are you, retired? Why don't you do something useful with your life and enjoy it, do some painting or write a book.

'I think mystery shopping is a waste of time - fancy coming on a Saturday. It's all about ticks in a box. Every salesman is different, each has a technique of selling that they're comfortable with, so as long as they do the job they get paid to do, we're all happy. Do we really need mystery shoppers like you hounding us every week. Just because some Dickhead thinks it helps us selling.' They were left stunned like someone had spoilt their game. We never saw or heard from them again, but we had others in their place.

Going back, they were moving from one dealership to

the other site. On the day of that move, we had a phone call - I took it.

'Good morning, my name's Wayne, you're through to sales, so how can I help?'

'Yes, good morning to you. I'm thinking of upgrading my car, so could you tell me what's the popular car everyone's going for in your dealership?'

Came the voice from this seventy-year-old man. His speech was shaky trying to keep up with breathing. I'm sure he was dribbling when he spoke.

'So you want me to go through every car we sell?'

'Only the best sellers.'

So after asking him what car he drove, I twigged that he wasn't a genuine buyer. He was reading from a script, so I went through the whole sales procedure, what make, model, how many doors, what colour he wanted, what was car for, work or pleasure? How many dogs has he got?

'Dogs. I don't have any dogs.'

'I thought you told me you had some dogs. So you don't need the car for dogs?'

'What's your name?'

'You want to know my name? My name is Mouch.'

'No it's not. I'm ordering you to give me your name, so what is your name?'

'Mister, I don't know who you are, but I don't have to tell you f' all. OK, my name is Gladstone.'

'That's not your name.'

'Why isn't that my name. OK, my name is Jock.'

'Look, I ask the questions here. I asked you for your name.'

'Why, so you can write it down and give it to my manager. You must think I'm off the banana boat. My name is Mr Turbo Diesel. If you like doing your job as a mystery shopper, go elsewhere and hound them. You've been rumbled. Now I'm going to deal with someone who wants to buy, not waste my time like you, so piss off.'

'I want to speak to your manager.'

'Well, call back.' I put the phone down. A few moments later, I heard...

'We haven't a Gladstone or Jock working here. Those were the names he gave you? Look, I'm the manager here, and I'm telling you we don't have anyone with those names here. Are you sure you have the right dealership?'

'Well, make sure your manager does hear about this. I couldn't give a toss what you say. I'm not going to be spoken to like that from you or anyone else.'

But then you always have the bottom feeder who will spend hours with these people just for the brownie points. Didn't he do well? Isn't he a good boy? He'll go out of his way to show them around a car knowing that he has no chance of selling them a car, but still tries his hardest to flog them that dead horse.

I remember a trainee salesman who had a mystery shopper turn up. Someone was telling me, she wanted to go out in some flash car the dealership had in their showroom. So he took all the lady's details, booked her a time, got the vehicle ready, then waited for her arrival. She turned up in a Mercedes, I think it was an E220 cabriolet.

He asked for the driving licence of the person who was

going to drive the car, and she duly obliged. He also got her home phone number, which, for her, was a big mistake. They went out on a test drive, came back, when she informed him that she will be in touch after she had sorted out the finance on the car she had driven. As the days went by, he phoned her up to see what was going on and when she was coming in with the money to purchase the car.

She said she would let him know. We could see he was wasting his time but we let him hound her for wasting his. For four weeks he phoned this lady up. He was getting nowhere. He sent her loads of letters. She ended up phoning the manager to complain about the young salesman harassing her every other day about buying a car.

Again, big mistake. The manager asked her, 'Did you have a test drive? Did you say that you were going to sort the finance out for the car?' to which she said, 'yes', and she was on a mystery shop all those weeks back and she had no intentions of buying a car.

'Well, you'll have to tell him that you're not buying, and you were wasting his time, because I'm not.'

Then he wished her a nice day.

12

The Vatman Who's Been at the Vat

Every business dreads the day when they say they're coming, even if the company books are straight and in order, they tend to find fault in every item of paperwork that they find. The element of suspicion and mistrust is around you and the place of work when they turn up for an inspection.

So when you receive the letter telling you that they have booked an appointment to visit on a said day, that's like throwing a spanner in the works. If the said date is inconvenient, please let them know to arrange a different time. Any day is inconvenient when they make an appointment, so it's not worth putting the day off. They're coming to see you anyway.

We had the letter informing us that a date had been set for a Friday in July, of all days a Friday. That's the start of the weekend. There is always a good atmosphere on a Friday. If we had a good week. we go out that night.

The VAT inspector is in the same league as the ex-copper who becomes an insurance claims assessor because he was shit in his last job, never got anywhere in his last career. Then there is the dentist, however friendly they are towards you, the ones who say, come in, smile, this won't hurt. Who the hell are they to tell you it won't hurt. They're the ones who are smiling when you leave in agony.

In six weeks, the man will be here. Then the start of the day of whispering starts. We don't want him to know what's going on with us. Helping the owner with what he needs doing, helps him get rid of his stress until the day the vat man arrives.

'Good morning, I'm here to see Mr Washington, my name's Harrington from Customs and Excise.'

'One moment, sir, I'll get him for you.'

'Before you do that, could you get me a glass of water, please?'

'OK, if you want to take a seat here, I'll get you your water.'

Working for a family-owned garage environment has its benefits. The pressure to sell is not as cut-throat as a main dealership and they appreciate every car that gets sold. You don't mind putting yourself out helping, selling more cars to keep everyone happy.

The layout is set differently. There are three sales desks, and the office is away from the sales and showroom in a room at the back of the building, so when either the bank manager or the advertising rep comes in, they have a bit of privacy.

So, after getting him his water, I went and got my boss.

'Frank, Mr Harrington the vat man is here. Would you like me to show him through?'

'No, I'll come out there, cheers Peter.'

'He won't be a minute, Mr Harrington.'

'Thanks.'

'Are you OK there?'

'No not really, I had a bit of a heavy night, last night.'

'Good morning, Mr Harrington. I'm Frank Washington,' the owner said, offering his hand of friendship.

'Morning, Mr Washington, I'm from Customs and Excise, here to do a check of your vat returns and other paperwork, so I might as well get started. Where would you like me to sit?'

'If you'd like to come through to my office, you will have some peace and quiet and be able to work here.'

'OK. thanks.'

As the owner sat him down at his desk, he came back into the showroom or salesroom. We can only get one car in here, so we have to call it something.

'You all right, Frank?' I asked.

'He seems a bit strange. Not your normal vat man. I expected him to be a short, fat, bald guy, an old man with thick-rimmed glasses.'

'The one that lives at home, either with his mummy or on his own. Well, this one's what, late twenties early thirties, looks like he wants to enjoy himself. Apparently he was on the piss last night - must have a bit of a hangover.'

'That means he will be here longer than he should.'

'Well, how long should he be here? Not all day, I hope.'

'I've known these bastards to take over some places. A friend of mine had them at his place once for three days. They took his place to pieces, never found anything, mind you. Pete, make a brew and I'll go and see if vat who been on the vat wants a coffee or tea.'

'I'm making a brew, Mr custom man. Do you fancy one?'

'Can I just have a glass of water? That might settle my headache.'

'What, did you have a bad night or something?'

'It was a mate of mine. He had a birthday yesterday so we went out last night to celebrate. We found a club and stayed there all night. I must have left there about three or something like that. Someone said it was the early hours of the morning, so I'm a bit the worse for wear.'

'Oh dear.'

'To be honest, I can't be arsed to do this. Can I ask for a favour? I have a birthday card for my brother, but don't have a stamp. Do you have a stamp I could have? I'll pay for it.'

'I'll give you a stamp, first or second?'

'How much does it cost to send a card to Australia?'

'Two first class stamps will get the card there.'

About half past, the guy went and had a kip in his car, then came back an hour later still suffering with his hangover.

'Mr Harrington, I see you're suffering with a bad head, so why don't you come to the pub and have a hair of the dog?' asked one of the salesmen.

'That sounds like a good idea. Where is the nearest pub? That might help.'

'Just down the road, about five minutes in the car. It's called the Red Planet. I'll give you a lift if you want.'

'Let me just finish what I'm doing here. I might as well have an early lunch, then try and come back with a clear head.'

So down to the nearest watering hole we went with our own VAT man. How cool was that? This guy had only been in the job for a few years, still trying to get used to it. He said he hated coming to the small places like this. Prefers going for the big fish - the ones who are taking the mickey. People who milk the system, and drive around in the flash cars. They don't like paying their dues that could run into hundreds of thousands of pounds.

'Those are the ones we are after, not the small fry like the showroom you're working at. I'll tell you what,' our vat man said, 'take me back to the site. I can't be bothered to work for the rest of the day. I know I should have had today off.'

So back to site we went, and piled through the doors. Our boss looked a bit shocked to see all his staff with this guy.

'If I could have my case, I'm going home. Here are your books, they're all in order. If you could sign this declaration, I will be gone. You won't hear from us for a while.'

'Well OK, as long as there will be no comeback.'

'That's all right, Mr Washington. Your book work's in order, the tax returns are in order. I cannot see there being any problems. I'll just sign this form and be on my way.'

'Sure, is that it then? Nothing else? Just sign this piece

of paper? Well, I hope your brother has a good birthday, and you have a good weekend.'

'Once I've slept this hangover off, I'll be right as rain.'

That was it. All that worrying for the last couple of weeks, wondering what to expect from this guy, and that was it. He had been out, got lagged up for the night.

We got a good tip at the end of the day from Mr Washington for getting the hair of the dog inside the VAT man. No-one has ever known this to happen, and I doubt they ever will.

13

You Can Pick Your Friends

'Hello, you're through to sales, my name's Greg, what can I do for you on this wonderful Tuesday?'

'I've never driven a Vauxhall before so I was just enquiring if you do Motobility?'

'Of course we do, but our specialist is off for a week. However, as we all help one another here, what can I do for you?'

'My renewal for my car is through. I have to get a new automatic car, so please tell me, do you have any small cars that can take a wheelchair in the boot?'

'Let me see, we have the Corsa or the Astra.'

'Well, are they big enough to place a wheelchair in the back?'

'Madam why not come into the showroom so that we can take it from there.'

'I'll do that. Your name's Greg, should I see you?'

'Please, if you come in today, I'll be waiting for you.

What is your name, mam, please?'

'Wilson.'

'OK, Mrs Wilson, I'll see what automatic cars we can show you. What time can you come in to our showroom today?'

'Say half an hour.'

'I'll be waiting for you.'

Sure enough, thirty minutes later Mrs Wilson and her family arrived at the showroom. It didn't take her long to get the wheelchair out of the car. Moments later she was wheeling herself around looking up and down to see what would suit her, and one that would take her wheelchair in the boot.

'Mrs Wilson, I'm Greg, thank you for coming in, nice to see the family as well. Are there any cars in the showroom that have caught your eye?'

'There is one - where is it? Dark red.'

'Astra or the Astra Estate, which one would you like to sit in? This one's the estate.'

'Well, it looks a bit on the large side.'

'It's slightly bigger than the Ford Fiesta, has more space than the Corsa, and you can have it in automatic.'

'I'd like to see how easy it is for my wheelchair to get in and out of the car, as well as myself.'

Just then my phone started to ring. 'Excuse me, Mrs Wilson, I just want to answer my phone.'

'OK, I just want to see if my wheelchair can fit in the boot.'

Little did I know that while I was on the phone, two members of her family had picked up Mrs Wilson and placed her on the floor. They placed her wheelchair in the boot, then walked off and sat in the car. It was only when I returned to the family that I could hear some groaning coming from somewhere near the car. That was when I found my customer, Mrs Wilson, rolling on the floor like a beached whale.

'I would like my chair out of the rear of this car, please. I'm getting out of here and coming back on my own. It's like this every time I go to look at a car with this lot. They take the piss. I'm the only one who can drive in this family, and this is the way they bloody treat me.'

The following week she returned, needless to say without her family, and purchased a car that satisfied her needs, Mum's Taxi.

14

Saturday Morning

'Sir, can I help you? I see you looking at these cars. Has any of them caught your eye?'

'No, I'm just looking.'

'OK, sir, give me a shout when you need some help.'

'Like I said, I'm just looking.'

Ten minutes later, another salesman passes by the same man and says the exact same thing, only to be told by this man, 'Christ! I'm only fucking looking, what harm am I doing just looking for a car?'

'Sorry, I was only wondering if I could help.'

'If I needed any help, I would come and see you, wouldn't I? Fuck me, you go into a supermarket, do they come up to you every two minutes and hound you - do they? If I knew what I wanted, I would be asking for the keys, wouldn't I?'

'OK, point taken.'

Our manager again walked past the same guy. It's

Saturday morning, a good day for selling cars. 'Are you all right, sir?' he asks. Big mistake.

'How many more of you are going to come up to me and ask if I'm all right? If I wasn't, I wouldn't be fucking here, would I? I'm fucking looking, nothing else, just looking, fuck me, if I had aids you'd be nowhere in sight, would you?'

'OK sir, I understand you're only looking. Well, do you mind going over the other side of the road to fucking look? Perhaps you might get a better view from there, thank you.'

The weather's lovely, a hot summer Sunday. We open all the showroom doors to let some fresh air blow through. It's going to be a quiet day. People will go down to the coast, not much going to happen today. I might as well get my chair and take it outside to soak up those sun rays. No doubt someone will ruin it.

Why does the odd Indian or Asian phone any showroom and ask about a car? You go through all the details, not leaving anything out. Will there be a part-exchange involved? The answer is usually no. Well it happened on that Sunday, getting ready to close. It must have been half past three when the family turned up.

'We want to buy a new car.'

They must think that by getting here at this time of the day they're going to get a better deal. It was the same people on the phone earlier. We're not a fucking supermarket, we don't reduce the price half an hour before closing.

'Are we buying today, sir?'

'If we get a good deal I think we might.'

'Well, if you would like to be seated at my desk, I'll see what I can do for you. As I said over the phone, I'll show you how I got to that price. So you want a five-door car in green, must be a 2.0 litre. That's how much it's going to cost you, then I take off the discount. That's the total price you have to pay, happy?'

'So what's your best price?'

'That is the best price'

'No, you can do better than that. Come on, give me your best price.'

One thing I learnt when dealing with these people, they love to barter. When they want something, they'll expect you to give it to them. So this is how you get around this situation. You get two price lists, last year's and this year's new price list. Show them the car at last year's price, then discount it at this year's price. They think they're making a saving of nearly two grand. When they see that, deal done.

'Good price, we all happy. I sign paper, give you deposit.'

Now you think that's the last you'll hear from them, that is until their car has turned up. Then you phone the customer and you tell them what's going on and when their car will be ready for delivery. You tell them the car will be here in two weeks.

Then the phone calls start. We've been out with friends, and they tell us we could get the car cheaper, so can you give me a better price on the car. I just knew this was going to happen.

'Sorry, I can't do that, you agreed on the price, the car's been ordered now.'

'Well, I might go to the other showroom and get more discount, but I don't want to do that, I want to use you.'

'I'll tell you what I'm going to do, sir. When I finish talking to you, I'm going to get you a cheque for your deposit, get it posted to you today, and cancel the order. That sounds good, doesn't it, so in other words you want me to cancel your order?'

'No, I don't want you to do that. I was just seeing if you could reduce the car price any more.'

'You people always want something for nothing. Well sorry, the car will be here in a couple of days. Do you want it, yes or no?'

'Yes'

'OK, I'll call when the car is here, goodbye.'

15

Don't Shoot the Driver

'Dennis, you live near Orpington, don't you?' asked the manager.

'No, I live miles away from that town.'

'But it's a route you can come to work on.'

'If I did a large detour, I suppose so. Why do you ask?'

'Well, tomorrow on your way to work, I want you to pick up a Ford Galaxy from a customer's house, swap your car for hers, and bring it back here where we can do the requirements to keep this lady off our backs. We blame the kids but the customer is always right, so they say. She accuses us for the lining coming off in her car. We will give you the address later, before you go home. If you get there just after nine, she should be back from the school run. This means you can have a little extra lay in bed. Aren't we good to you?'

'Who's got a map I can borrow to find the road I've got to go to?'

'There's one in the reception desk drawers,' someone piped up.

'I live here, but that looks miles away. The morning traffic might have eased by then. I'll leave home at eight. What's the people like, Steve? Will I get a cup of tea?'

'No, she is one miserable old bitch. She has been on the phone every day for the past two weeks, nagging to get the work done on her car. Cup of tea from her? She would more likely give you her kids' piss. All you have to do is just give her your car, take hers, and come back here. Don't get involved with any slanging match. The quicker you're back, the quicker she can have her Ford back.'

So, the next day, 'Have a good day, love,' as I kissed my other half goodbye. 'I'll give you a call during the day.'

Off I set. There seems much more traffic this time of the morning on the motorway. Perhaps that's why I leave that little bit earlier. I'm sure everyone leaves their homes at the same time to go to work. Mr Brown is leaving for work, I think I'll join him. Ah! Mr Brown and Mr Jones are leaving for work, I think I'll join them. It goes on and on, that's my theory of the morning rush hour. I arrived at the address with fifteen minutes to spare, wondering how far away the school was, or would she go shopping and make me wait that little bit longer for whatever reason? Twenty minutes later, the Galaxy turns up and out steps a rather plain looking lady. I thought women liked to tart themselves up to do the school run, obviously not in this case.

'Good morning,' I said in my usual cheerful way.

'It fucking will be when you sort this car out, won't it?'

'Oh, like that, is it?'

'Well, you would be if you'd paid out all that money for a pile of shit. First it was the paintwork, so we sent it back for that to be done, then the fucking idiots who worked on it sent it back with the fucking screws missing, the ones that hold the lining up to the roof, so back it's got to go, nothing but fucking problems since we've had it.'

'Sorry to hear about that, madam. What's the chance of a cup of tea?'

'Look, haven't you got to be going? The quicker you go, the quicker we can have our vehicle back, so here's the keys to the Galaxy, and I've got to drive that piece of shit. How am I going to get all the kids in that?'

'Hopefully, it's only for one day and you'll get it back tomorrow, all in working order.'

'I doubt it, so I won't hold my breath. If I see it tomorrow, all well and good, OK, ta ra.'

No wonder they wanted me to do this job. Anyone else would have told her to fuck off. Myself, I'm nice and calm, never let anything bother me until the day I meet this old hag. I got the vehicle back to the garage within an hour, which wasn't bad going, only to be told that the woman had phoned, telling my manager that I was rude to her, saying to them that I told her she shouldn't have bought the piece of shit anyway. That was a big lie. I never said anything of the sort, so that's pissed me off for the rest of the day. What an evil old wench.

'You know I had to pick that Galaxy up this morning,' I said to my wife, as we had a chat on the phone, 'somehow she has dropped me in the shit for some unknown reason.

I'll tell you more about it when I get home - what's for dinner, love?'

'Whatever you fancy.'

'Skip dinner then, ha! ha! must go, see you later, love you, bye.'

'Dennis, the car will be ready for you to take back to the customer when you go home.'

'OK boss, I won't say fuck all to her, I'll just give her the keys and I'm on my way.'

So the car turns up. One thing I hadn't noticed before was the amount of crap on the floor, sweet wrappers, the mud from the football boots, reading books, and the odd tissue. What a state to leave your car in. You can't begin to imagine the place they live in. It must be a pigsty, but that's not my problem.

That afternoon, the husband came into the garage to see how the work went on the vehicle. It was only a couple of screws that needed to be put in the ceiling.

What is it with people with money, do they think that they own everyone, snap their fingers and we all come running? I don't, so when some pratt asks me to make them a cup of tea without saying please, it makes you do things that you shouldn't do, like wee in it, or make it really strong, gob in it as well. You can guess which one I did. The guy never said thanks. How much do manners cost? - Nothing. They must be of royal blood. I hate people like that. You can imagine what the children will turn out like, not my problem.

'You might as well go now, Dennis, miss all that rush hour traffic,' said my manager. 'We'll see you tomorrow.'

'Sure, Steve, going to miss the beer after work. What does that bloke do for a living, if I may ask?'

'I think he imports exotic fruit like bananas. That's how he makes his money - his wife just sits at home and spends it.'

'I thought he owned the place, the way he orders everyone about. He didn't even say thanks for the tea.'

'You meet that type of people in this trade. They all want something, so you have to let it go over your head. Don't let it get you down. We end up getting our own back anyway. I won't tell you how much we made on that deal, but we keep a little back in case the car needs any work doing to it after a vehicle has left the site.'

'Sure, no doubt I'll get caught somewhere - road works or a smash, just to hold up the flow of traffic. Should take an hour and a bit to get to my destination.'

'Or the pub,' a colleague offered.

'Not until I've dropped the car off at that old moose's house.'

Off I set, doing the rat run, the quickest route to the A21, that's if there is one, with all these speed bumps. Is it really worth the hassle of taking short cuts? I suppose it is.

The drive was going quicker than I thought, so I decided to stop at a pub just off Bromley Common, The Ramblers Rest, for a swift pint, have that, then I'll be back on my way. There I spied a little object on the grass bank that someone had discarded. That might come in handy I thought to myself. I whip a tissue from my pocket. While no-one was looking, I quickly picked it up, wrapped the object into the tissue, then put it in my pocket. I downed my beer and made my way back to the vehicle.

I opened the door, thinking where to put this used thing. I know, with sneering grin, I placed my find on the floor under the front driver's seat, slightly showing but not showing enough to spot straight away. Everybody has an evil streak, and mine came out that day.

The school run must be over by now, as I waited outside this house for about thirty minutes. I could have stayed at the pub and had another refreshment, rather than wait there for happy features to turn up. Hooray! About fucking time, I said to myself.

'Hi there, Mrs Malone, one Ford Galaxy with all the work done, well what ever needed to be done. Would you like to inspect it, then I can go?'

'OK, let me dump the shopping indoors first.'

'Sure, I'll just wait here then.' What, is she putting it all away? She's sure taking the piss, but then I know I'm never going to see this couple again, am I?'

'Well, show me what they've done then. It was inside on the ceiling at the back of the car.'

'Sure, let's just open the boot for you, put the key in, turn to the left, click, here we go, there you have it - repair work done, I hope.'

'Why couldn't they do that in the first place? Yea, it will do. Here are your keys.'

'Thanks.'

I heard some months later that the couple were going through a bad patch in their marriage. She was accusing him of having an affair, and he thought she was. The couple had decided to clean their cars out, and he had found a used Johnny under the seat in the Galaxy car.

'Well, she's the one who mainly drives it,' he told my manager when he was making a courtesy phone call to ask if there were any problems with the car.

She shouldn't have said those nasty things to me, I said to myself.

16

If Only You Knew What I Meant

'Thank you for calling. You need wheels, we do the deals, my name's Ryan, how can I help you?'

'My name's Mrs James, me and my boyfriend, well he's in hospital having an operation today - you still got our money? You know what I mean?'

'No.'

'Well, we came there three weeks ago, do you know what I mean? We were going to get a car, yer, we didn't so we want our money back, you know what I mean?'

'Sorry, but why do you keep saying, do I know what you mean? If I knew what you meant, I would know what you mean. You're telling me you came in here three weeks ago to buy a car. Did you get credit?'

'I don't know, but we didn't buy a car so my boyfriend asked me to ask for our money back, you know what I mean?'

'Can you shut up saying, do I know what you mean? How much was your deposit?'

'Three hundred and fifty pounds, you know what I mean?'

'So you gave a deposit of three hundred and fifty pounds, and they haven't sent it back to you. Do you remember who the salesman was so I can find out what happened to your money?'

'I think he was a little bloke, you know what I mean? Yer, we were here for about three hours, you know what I mean?'

'Yes, I know what you mean.'

'I think his name was Mick, but I'm not sure, you know what I mean? It may have been someone else.'

'If you wouldn't mind waiting a minute, I'll find out where it is, then try and get it sent to you, or find out what has happened to it. So excuse me, if you know what I mean?'

'OK then, mate.'

'Dean, I've a lady here on the phone. She's wanting her deposit back, name's James. They came in about three weeks ago, never bought a vehicle. She's come up with some bullshit about her other half having an operation today. She seems very common - you na what I mean, mate?'

'I remember them, a pair thick as shit - time wasters. They were here for about three hours, just kept messing. Who was the salesman?'

'I'm sure it was one of Peter's,' came the reply from my manager. 'I'm sure they live locally as well if I recall. They let their kids run riot, pissed the other people off who were here. How much deposit did they leave?'

'Three hundred and fifty pounds.'

'Wait a moment. I'll find out if we have any money to give her.'

'Sure. Mrs James, sorry to keep you waiting. My manager is sorting something out now, try not to keep you for much longer.'

A couple of minutes later my manager returns with a broad smile on his face.

'If she can get her herself down here now, DP said he'll pay her out.'

Some ten minutes later, I return to the phone, 'Mrs James I found out what happened to your deposit. The salesman Peter who was helping you, told me on that Saturday night they went down the pub with your deposit and pissed it up against the wall, you know what I mean? Only joking, if you get yourself... hello, hello. Oh, she's put the phone down, I was going to tell her to get down here now and we'll give her money back, but she hung up. Ah well, I'm sure she'll phone back some day.

Twenty minutes later, three men turn up with baseball bats wanting to take the salesman's head off if they didn't get their money within five minutes. Funny, this was the guy who was having an operation sometime this morning. I've never known anyone to make a recovery that quick, and he could even run.

'Who's the pratt taking the piss out of my girlfriend? She phoned about twenty minutes ago trying to get my fucking dosh back, so you've got two fucking minutes to give it to me or I'll take someone's head off.'

'Just wait there and I'll get the manager,' the guy who met them said, crapping himself. He then legged it upstairs to the office. 'There's a fucking mad man downstairs, wants to take someone's fucking head off if he doesn't get his deposit back.'

'I'll go and see him. Obviously this wanker hasn't got a sense of humour, has he Ryan?'

I love it when our manager gets angry, especially because he comes from the midlands, and they hate us southerners. The argument lasted half an hour. The pykies got their funds back and that was the excitement over for that day. I was told to be nice to people on the phone when I talk to them. Bollocks, if they can't speak properly over the phone, that's their problem.

17

The Non-Going Convertible

Not every showroom has a receptionist who doesn't like answering the phone. Well that's what they're paid for, isn't it?

The receptionist we had would answer every other call. We would sometimes watch her, and were convinced she held the phone to her mouth and pretended she was talking to someone. Every time there was an incoming phone call, she would go for a walkabout, so the sales staff would have to pick up the phone and answer it themselves.

'Somebody get that phone. Where's the receptionist?'

'On one of her usual walkabouts,' I called out. 'I'll get it. Good morning, my name's Tony, how can I help you?'

'Good morning can I have a sales, please?'

'You're through to sales. How can I be of assistance to you?'

'Yer, I a normally talk to Alan, he a helps me to a get what a car I need.'

'Sorry, Alan is not in today, what's your name please, so I know whom I'm talking to.'

'Sure, you see my name's Luigi and a Alan he a been at a your place for a long a time so he a knows a my problem. It's a my hip. OK, you have a one of those 206 convertibles in a the showroom no, I wanna know a how a long does it a take to get a one if I order today?'

'A new convertible will take between 8-12 weeks.'

'8-12 weeks a, I tell you a what I'm a gonna do. I'm a coming there, you a take my order for da car no? So I be there in half an hour, Luigi gonna buy me a 206, Tony, I see you then, OK?'

'OK, whatever.'

'You what a, why you a say that. I say I'm coming in, I'm gonna be there, so I see you a soon OK no.'

'Sure,' putting the phone down. Who's upset him, he's going to be an arsehole to deal with.

'Joe, I've one of Alan's old customers coming in to look at the 206 convertible.'

'What's his name, Tony?'

'Luigi Roffie.'

'I remember him, he has a dodgy hip. He has bought three cars in the last year for members of his family. They all work for him so he likes to look after them. He's a nice chap, the man will buy the car if he likes it.'

So he turned up, Mr ice cream seller, the Italian stallion with a limp, himself.

'Good morning, you must be Mr Roffie.' I introduced myself to him as he walked through the showroom. 'My name's Tony.'

'How are you, Tony, dis the car 206 yes? What engine is in dis car?'

'2.0 litre petrol. They also do a 1.6 as well.'

'Show me how a the roof it a works.'

'If you come this way, this is the boot, push the button, up comes the lid. This is the inside of the boot, to have the roof down you must have this protected screen pulled across or the roof will not close.'

Taking a look around the car. 'This way, Mr Roffie, please have a seat. In the car you have two levers either side on these pillars, you uncouple them like so, then see that switch on the consul there. We have the roof down in three minutes, and the lid is tucked away in the boot. As you can see there's not much room in the back for passengers. They should have made it into a two-seat car.'

'I see you have a one of a them out a side, you a take me for a drive, yes?'

'Well, it's the manager's car. I'll go and get the keys, so I'll meet you by the car.'

'Joe may I borrow your car and keys to take Mr Roffie on a test drive? We'll only go around the block.'

'Sure Tony, just around the block, don't go too mad.'

'No worries, boss. This way, Mr Roffie, would you like to drive?'

'No thanks a Tony you a drive.'

So off they go, roof down like a couple of posers, on the test drive. The good thing about driving one of these cars is it does turn heads, so when you drive through a town centre you know more people will be in the showroom to look at this car. Ten minutes later they're back, the car's parked up, Mr Roffie is sitting at the salesman's desk going through a brochure, selecting what colour, the engine size, then orders the car he wants.

The manager then gets to work on his computer, punching in all the details. The reply comes back telling him that the car will be built on a certain day and date, and will be delivered in three months.

'Your car will be here in about 12 weeks. It might be earlier but that's the date they've given us.'

'That's a all right, I give you say a four thousand a pounds deposit, OK?'

'That's fine. I'll get you your order, receipts for your deposit, and what car you're going to get. This will take a few moments.'

Remember I said he had a dodgy limp!

NINE WEEKS LATER

'Time to make that phone call, Tony. Tell Mr Roffie his convertible will be here on a transporter and delivered here by Monday, so we need to give a reg number so he can get the car insured and we can tax his vehicle.'

'Hello, is Mr Roffie there. It's Tony from Wingates.'

'Yes a it's a me, what can I a do for you?'

'Sir, your car was built earlier. The car is going to be with us on Monday. So we need to get the car registered, taxed for when you pick the car up, so, if you're sitting comfortably, we will give three registration numbers, and ask you to pick one so it can go on your car.'

'Sure, I'll a do that now, you a give me the three numbers and I'll see which a I a like.'

He picks one of the numbers. We then register the car

in his name, get it ready for Thursday, the day he said he wants the car. He brought his insurance in on Tuesday so we showed him his car. The car is up on the ramp with one of the technicians working on it.

'There's your lovely vehicle, Mr Roffie. They're making sure everything is roadworthy.'

'I forgot it was a blue, I a like a this.'

'There you have it, sir. Your vehicle will be ready for you on Thursday, is that OK?'

'Thursday is fine. I a bring a building society cheque and cap to save my a hair from a blowing off, ha! ha!'

'OK, see you Thursday, Mr Roffie.'

'Thanks a Tony, see you Thursday.'

With that we shook hands, and on his way he went, only for him to return in a couple of days, all exciting stuff.

Thursday was hand-over day for my Italian pizza man. In he came nice and early, the eager beaver.

'Good morning and what a nice morning it is, Mr Roffie. You'll be driving home with the roof down and the sun in your face? I wish it was me taking the car.'

'Good a morning to you this a beautiful day a.'

'If you come this way, sit yourself down here. We can do the paperwork, then I'll show you around the car.'

Everything signed, so out to the car we go. I went first. Mr Roffie, the customer, followed with his limp.

'This a Peugeot 206 2.0 convertible in metallic blue and it's yours, so if you would like to sit yourself in the driving seat, then I'll go through the switches, buttons, and knobs so you'll know how the car works.'

'Tony, I think a we have a big a problemo?'

114

'What's the problem, Mr Roffie?'

'It's a lovely car, de colour, the sport dials, de wheels, it's abella, but it's a notta bloody automatic, I notta drive this a car, it's a no a bloody good a to me. I a can only drive an automatic, I thought you knew I have a to have an automatic.'

'Oh shit!!! No one told me that's what you needed. I'll go and see my boss. Oh Shit!!'

'Joe, we have a big problem with Mr Roffie. He wanted an auto. That car out there is manual. He needs an auto for his hip problem. What the fuck are we going to do about it?'

'Give him his money back. They don't even make that car in an auto. Where is the man? I'll go and talk to him. I'll have to use my management charm.'

So after an hour and a half of haggling and *mama mias* from Mr Roffie, he left in a taxi, but not before he had committed himself to another ten grand on top of what he had spent, on a 607 auto. In the pub after work, we were sitting down talking about that day's event, the manager, myself, and two other salesmen.

'You were bloody lucky, Tony, with that Mr Roffie. I thought we were going to lose that deal, but I've got to tell you this, we made more money on that deal alone than any other car that we've sold this month.

'So our dwarf dealing principal tried to get in on the act. He said he was going to sell a car today. A couple came in with no part-exchange involved, he sold them a car at a loss - a big loss, the idiot has to get involved, I wish he'd fuck off - the wanker.'

'Thanks for your help, boss, you saved the day.'

18

The Dealer Killer Principal

The dealer killer, the dealer principal himself. Now this man can wipe out in seconds the hours of hard work someone has done. You would have thought our D.P worked for the garage down the road, because when he had fucked our customers off, they would go down the road there and buy their new car from them, which often happens. I remember I sold a new car to a young family. They had their parents with them. The deal took about 45 minutes from start to them signing. The dad said, 'I'd like one of those cars...' 'come back, say Wednesday, and I'll value your car, give you a good price, Johnny, then we'll take it from there.'

'We will do that, say 3 o clock,' the father said.

Wednesday came, they turned up, I got my manager to underwrite their car. He gave them a good price, he did, because the customer - he smiled. Unfortunately he was called away so they said they would be back the next day to sign up. The trouble was that Thursday was my day off, so my manager said he would finish it off for me. Now that's all right, I knew he would do, so I left them in safe hands.

But somehow, the wanker of a dealer principal got hold of them. They didn't sign up. They phoned the next day to say, 'we were talked out of buying a car, sorry - goodbye.'

Another time was when I gave someone a price for their car that they were going to part exchange. I thought that was a good price, only to be asked to phone the customer and tell her that we've offered her five hundred pounds too much for her car. Too right I'm going to pass that message on, ain't I? No, that's that mug's doing. He had to sort it out, he's a fucking nightmare.

Monday morning was the best morning of the week, THE SALES MEETING, when we all had to sit around and listen to this fucking idiot telling us that we are all world war one fighter pilots, that every time a customer came on to the forecourt, we were to go out, circle around and corner them, then shoot them down. In other words, don't let them leave without buying a car. We had to be told this every poxy Monday - what a waste of twenty minutes. If we could sell bullshit, then this man would be mega rich. We're all re-born salesmen, we love the job, we all have no other outlook apart from selling cars. Well sorry, but just sitting at a desk is so boring, waiting for someone to buy a car is as dull as watching paint dry.

I had a friend tell me his dealer principal would hide behind trees just to listen to his sales technique, weird pratt. If you're selling the cars, isn't it best to let the sales team get on with it? If it ain't broke, don't try to fix it, so they say. Like I was saying, some dealer principals haven't got an idea between them. The money they're on, the car they drive, it just makes you wonder what they do all day?

'Johnson, in my office now. What's this, you told a customer to fuck off? I've got a fax from a manufacturer telling me that you've to say you're sorry.'

'Bollocks, I'm not saying anything to him, he wanted something for nothing. The paint was coming off his car through stone chips. He told me to get it done. I said, who's going to pay for it? because I'm not, so he took the car, came back Wednesday, demanding that I get the work done on his car. So I told him to fuck off.'

'Nice one, Mark, leave it with me. In future, if you feel like telling someone to go, tell them in a nice sort of way.'

He was the good type of dealer principal. He looked after his workforce, not like one Dealer Principal I knew and worked for. A man phoned up. He has a 306 estate that he wants to part-exchange, so the event went.

'Mark speaking, how can I help?'

'I have a 306 estate that I want to part-exchange. I'm looking to get a larger estate, 406 perhaps, so what would you give on my car - it's a Peugeot?'

'Can I stop you there, sir. I can't give you a price over the phone. You will have to bring your car in so I can get it underwritten. I'm here until seven tonight, so bring your car in and I'll gladly sort you a car out. Is that all right, sir.'

'I'll try and get there tonight.'

'OK sir, what's the name, please?'

'Graham Porter.'

'Thank you, Mr Porter. If you come in I'll be waiting for you. My name's Mark.'

'OK Mark, I'll see you, bye.'

At 5.30, a blue 306 drives through our gates into our parking bay. The driver makes his way towards the showroom, where there's just myself and another salesman.

'Here to see Mark. He's going to give me a price on my car.'

'Sure, I'll get him for you. Your name, please sir?'

'Mr Porter.'

'There's a Mr Porter here for you, Mark.'

'Hello, Mr Porter, thanks for coming in. Would you like a tea or coffee while I have a look at your car?'

'No thanks.'

'OK, I'll get an appraisal form. With this, I can show my manager in the morning, so may I have your car keys please?' Quick drive up and down the road, check the mileage, the odd scratch.

'So how much are you looking for, Mr Porter, on your car? Four to five grand.'

'If you could give me six to six and a half grand, I'll be happy.'

'If that's what you want, I'll see if I can get it for you, OK. What I'll do is give my manager a call, see if he can give a price over the phone. He's the man with the bible.'

Ten minutes of trying to get hold of the manager, with his phone engaged, was a waste of my time.

'Sorry, Mr Porter, I cannot get hold of my manager, so I'll have to leave it until tomorrow, then give you a call during the day.'

'OK, so a brand new 406 estate 1.8 is what, twelve grand, take off my six and a half grand - you're looking at five and a half to pay, OK. I'll wait for your call tomorrow.'

With that, Mr Porter went on his way. I said to the other salesman there, 'Did you hear me give him a price?'

'No I didn't.'

'That's all right, I don't know where he got that from.'

The next day I gave the appraisal form to the boss, 'this guy wants six to six and a half grand for his car. I said I would see what I could do,' passing the form to him to read.

'What's it drive like?'

'It drives OK, the odd stone chip, other than that it's a clean car.'

'Let's have a look in the Glass's guide,' finding the page, 'here it is. It books at four to four and a half. How much did he want?'

'Six to six and a half grand.'

'He's way out, so I'm going to offer him four grand.'

So I go and phone him to tell him the good news.

'Hi Mr Porter, I've just been with my manager to get you a good price for your car. He has had a look at the appraisal which I did last night, and said your car is worth four thousand pounds.'

'Four thousand, you said six and a half thousand.'

'No I never. I didn't give you a price. I said I'd have to wait until tomorrow to see my manager.'

'OK, I'll be in touch, Thanks, Mark.'

'OK, Mr Porter. I'll be waiting for your call.' That was it, well that's what I thought.

The next day I am summoned to my manager's office. 'That Mr Porter is going to take the company to court.'

'What the hell for, may I ask?'

'Did you price his car up last night, then tell him his car was worth six and a half grand?'

'No, I appraised his car and tried to get you on the phone last night, but couldn't, your phone was engaged, so I told him I'll get a price in the morning when you got here, which I did.'

'Well, you write a statement out so if he does take us to court, you're covered.'

'So you're going to stand by me, are you?'

'Just write the statement out to save yourself from going to court.'

'Bollocks, I'm not doing that. He wanted six to six and a half grand and I said nothing - his word against mine. Like it or lump it, sorry. Let him take us to court. Do I look bothered?'

'Just write out a statement, OK! If he takes us to court, you'll lose your job.'

'Nice to know that you'll stand by your staff.'

'Look, you offered him six grand odd, that's all.'

'I never offered him jack shit, so that must be that saying about the customer's always right. I never gave him any price. The guy's a roach. He's trying it on, he wants something for nothing.'

I might as well talk to myself, save my breath, this dealer principal is thick as shit. He never took me to court. I know I was right, but could never work for that idiot again, so I left.

19

Sorry! But Welcome to our Club

When a new salesman joins the sales team, there's dubious feeling towards him. The team will try their hardest to make him not welcome. First they'll be nice, asking the 'where were you before?' question, if you want a tea or coffee, you can use this, need to borrow a pen, calculator, appraisal form, but as soon as Joe de vehicle walks onto the site, does that sales team change. That's a finance deal, a used car with a bonus. He's a walking pound sign. No new man is going to have him - everyone for themselves. It's a good job it's not a sinking ship, because women and children would have to give a donation before leaving the ship. We all go through it, and we all do it to others, dog eat dog.

My sales manager came up to me. 'We've had a phone call from a guy who knows you, asking if there are any vacancies, so I've invited him down for an interview.'

'What's his name?'

'Marcus.'

'Palmer Turner, the stomper, if I can't get my own way I'll throw my toys.'

'Yes, you know the guy, well he'll be in later today about 5 o'clock, so if you want to say hello, stay a while.'

'I'll say hello if I see him, other than that you can talk to him.'

'What's up, Ginger, don't you like him?'

'I'm not saying a word. All I'll say is that I've worked with the two-faced twat.'

The next day.

'How did that Marcus get on last night, Del?' I asked the manager.

'He's full of shit, you could smell it a mile away, said he flew planes in the navy, so what the hell's he selling cars for? Well, I said we will be in touch but that idiot DP was still here late last night. He also had a chat with him and offered him a job.'

'The DP offered him a sales job. What a pratt! If I told you what he was like, I don't think you would have employed him, but it's not my company so you do what you have to do. He was my manager in the last place I worked. He was fucking useless. He can't make a decision without getting everyone involved. The other salesmen took the mickey. They used to go round to each other saying, do you like me, go on tell me you like me. When we dealt with people, and you did the deal on your own, it was classed as a full deal. When you closed them on your own, it was worth 75 pounds for the first ten deals, 150 pounds for each full deal after that. I did all right. I took home over two grand a month.

'Most of his deals were all half deals worth 35 pounds. I had to close most of his deals just to make him some money. The idiot went on to become a manager, but he needed help with every deal. No respect from the workforce, and now he's coming here to work. Del, if I said to you what ever you do, don't employ him, would you have listened to me?'

'Ginger, I've even told our dealer principal not to take him on. I do what you say, I said he's not what we need. Blame that wanker over there, mate.'

We had a good crew in our showroom. There were only the three salesmen, which was enough. We all work together, covering each other on our days off. When we've finished work for the day, an hour in the watering hole, then off home, an enjoyable place to work, living in each other's pockets, borrowing one another's car when we wanted. All good friends - until that Monday.

'So where's Phil?' we asked that Monday.

'He was told to go last Saturday,' our sales manager told us in the sales meeting office that morning. 'He, the DP, wants to tell you about the good news today. He'll be over in a minute, he wants the sales meeting to be at nine.'

'So we got rid of a good bloke, part of our team. Don't tell me for that there Marcus.'

'Looks that way,' our sales manager said.

'Bastard, I'm not going to help him this time. This is the real world.'

'Well, if you do that Ginger, I'm going to do the same. He gets no help from me.'

'OK Tony, we'll think of something.'

The sales meeting was a bit over the top that morning. Our dealer principal blowing his trumpet about how well we're going to perform now we have got another salesman joining us today. Little did he know he was one of the worst guys you could ever employ.

'Ginger, I've a plan up my sleeve. I have a man who wants a car.'

'When is he coming in?'

'Wednesday.'

Marcus took over Phil's table, or as we call it, dead man's desk. That Monday was quite a relaxed day for our new bloke. We showed him what was what, where things were kept, and he made himself at home so to say.

'I think I'm going to enjoy myself here, he informed me. It's a nice site they have here. It's better than working for Skoda. I should get a better car here as well, beats working where we worked at - you need wheels, we do deals. They were shit cars, weren't they?'

'That was a shit company. You went on to become a manager. They went bust, that says it all.'

'Hey Ginger, there's a phone call for you.'

'Coming Tony, talk to you later, Marc.'

'Not really, mate, just knew you needed to get away from him,' said Tony, as I reached for the phone.

'Cheers mate, you did me a favour.'

As the weeks went by, Marcus was trying to settle in. We hate bottom feeders and we had one here.

'That new guy is getting right on my nerves. Every time the telephone rings, he's on the case trying to nick our deals, hoping it's an enquiry. Remember I told you I had a customer coming in? Well, he will be here about 12.30 for a test drive. It's a Mondeo and it's a company purchase. They're not buying the rep a car for six months, so he just wants to try the car out to see how it feels. I'll be on my lunch hour. Do you think you could look after him, Ginger?'

'I'll tell you what, ask the new boy to help you. Better still, don't say a word. As soon as I see anyone entering the showroom I'll make a phone call or do something else. Leave it with me, Tony.'

Just after 12.30, a man came into the showroom. Looking at the man, he could have passed off as one of us, smartly dressed. 'I phoned earlier this morning, so I'm here looking for Tony,' mentioning he was hoping for a test drive, and the company he was working for was going to purchase him a car.

'Tony's not here sir, may I be of assistance to you?'

'Well I was hoping to drive the new Mondeo, the 2-litre diesel saloon.'

'Sure, give me five minutes, I'll have the car ready for you. What's your name please?'

'Mr Johnson. I've heard good reports about this car.'

'Car's ready, sir. If you would like to come this way. Going on a test drive, I'll be back in about ten minutes.'

'Take as long as you like, just sell a car,' came the reply from the manager's office.

They came back.

'Marc, tell us, how did you get on?'

'All right I think, he's just on the phone to his company, we might have a deal here.'

'Mr Johnson, would you like a tea or coffee?'

'Tea, please.'

Minutes later, they were both around the dead man's desk, going through the car brochures.

'So you like the car?'

'It was a nice drive. I would like to get one of those.'

'So when do you want to place an order with us? The colour you want, the engine size, I can get one for you in two weeks.'

'No thanks, Marcus, like I told the other salesman earlier this morning when I booked the test drive, it would be a company purchase. They're going to get me a car in six month's time. Then they'll purchase it from the internet to save on the cost.'

You could hear the salesman's mind yelling BASTARDS.

'There you have it, Marcus, thank you for the test drive. Now I've got to make my way back north where I live, thanks again - goodbye.'

'Marcus, give young Steve a hand to re-arrange the cars on the forecourt. He has the keys with him. With the pair of you doing it, it shouldn't take you too long,' said the manager.

'Sure,' came the reply.

'Ginger, there's a sales call. Can you take it?'

20

The Welder

What you shouldn't say to a salesman!

'Hello, Gordon speaking, how can I help you?'

'Just reading your ad in the paper. I know I've got bad credit so I need some help in getting a car. How do I go about it?'

'What's your name, please sir?'

'Jonathan, Jonathan Williams.'

'OK Jonathan, where in the country do you live?'

'Essex.'

'Do you have a full-time job, full UK driving licence, and a place to rest your head of a night time?'

'Yes, I've got all of them.'

'So when can you come to Kent or Surrey?'

'Can I come in today? I need a newer car than the piece of shit I'm driving now. The car's on its last legs.'

'Well, let me get you some finance first, which will take about an hour. Do you have today off?'

'Yer, that's why I'm phoning you now. I really need a car, pal.'

'I'll give you our address. You'll need to bring with you, your bank statements, proof of address, driving licence, wage slips, oh, and telephone bill, all in the last three months. Can you do that?'

'I can do that. What nice cars have you got there - any BMWs?'

'Yes, we have those cars here, but let me get you a line of finance open, Jonathan, and those vehicles are about ten grand.'

'If you get me finance, mate, I can afford it.'

'We'll see, right, get yourself down here now. It's going to take you about an hour, so if you leave Essex now, then I will have a line open for you by the time you get here. Do you have a mobile phone number I can have?'

'I've got three. I'll give you this one: 077... You can get me any time on that number.'

(Now, does this guy think we're going to have a sexual relationship, and I'm going to be his lover? Well, he is in for a shock, because between the time he gets here and the time he leaves, he's going to be my meat, putty in my hands. He'll do what I say, then he'll go home when I let him).

'Gordon, your Mr Williams has been accepted by one of the finance houses.'

'How much are they going to let him borrow?'

'£4000.'

'£4000? He's not going to be happy with that amount. Mr Flash wanted to buy a beamer. This will be fun, he'll have to make do with a Honda Civic.'

So an hour later, Mr Williams arrives in his piece of shit. He's then seated upstairs - all his documents are taken off him and photocopied.

'So Mr Williams, what line of work do you do?'

'My line of work. I stick metal to metal for a car company.'

'That seems a boring job, lifting pieces of metal all day.'

'It's a good job, I start at 7 in the morning, finish at 3 in the afternoon. If I want overtime, it's there. If you're prepared to work, the money is there, so how much can I borrow?'

'At the moment, four thousand pounds, but after seeing your wage slips, my manager is trying to get you more. So you're a welder, that's what I do as well, but it's a bit different to what you do.'

'Gordon, the manager would like to see you,' came the voice from another salesman.

'This could be what we've been waiting for, so I won't be a minute.'

'Your Mr Williams, the fucking roach, doesn't like paying anyone back, so he's going to have to take the four grand. Can you see what type of dippa he's got? You're looking at six grand if he wants a BMW. That will break the twat's heart, so go out there and nail him to a car he doesn't want. I'd like to see him gone in one hour. Fucking BMW, he's got more chance of a wank from the Pope than getting one of those.'

'OK boss, let us see what Mr "I earn more than you", gets out of this.'

'Jonathan, we've got all the replies back from the other finance companies. Only one is prepared to lend you any money, and they will only lend you £4000. So if you want a flash car, it's going to cost you that plus a deposit of £5000 or £6000. Do you have that kind of money? If they see a large deposit, then they'll lend you more money.'

'Oh, so what kind of car are we talking about?'

'How much deposit can you afford without getting yourself in debt?'

'Well, there's my car outside.'

'We'll give you a grand for that.'

'I can give you another grand, so that's two. Tell me, what car are we looking at?'

'Come with me Jonathan, I'll show you.'

This is the easy part. We take them to the warehouse, which has about seventy cars. Show them three cars, and you know they'll pick one of them. So the art is to show two cars out of their price range and the third they should go for. This was not the case with Mr Williams. He didn't like any of the cars. He had his brain locked on a BMW. So, like a spoilt little boy, started throwing his toys. My question must have fallen on deaf ears.

'Look, I've seen the cars you've shown me but they're not what I want. You have two cars I know I can afford, so can't I have one of those.'

'Let me go and have a word with my manager, I can only try.'

'Boy, is this guy thick, I've shown him the cars he can afford, but no, he wants either the MR2 or the Golf GTI. Is it a no, boss?'

'Let's have a look at his paperwork. Well, he earns good money. I'll make a phone call and try to get his limit raised.'

'What about spreading it over five years as well? That must help the case. I can feel a weld coming on.'

'Go and sit with your customer, this will take about five minutes. Just keep him happy, build up that desire for him to pay four hundred a month.'

'Well Gordon, how's it going, is there any joy with your boss?'

'He's on the phone as we speak, trying to get the limit raised.'

'So Jonathan, I take it the car is to pull birds and to impress your mates?'

'Something like that. I've had that old Honda for at least four years now so it was time for a change. I went to the local dealership to see about a new car, and that's when I found out I had a bad credit history. Fuck knows how I got it, they never told me.'

'They are not allowed to tell us. We tell everyone it could be a small debt that never got paid off. But it still fucks you up when you want something, mobile phone, car, even a mortgage. But if we get you this loan and you pay it back, your credit will be re-instated. You'll get finance offers every day, and you'll soon get pissed off with them.'

'Gordon, we have an answer, so can you just come back into the office,' Peter the finance manager requested.

'What's up Peter?'

'Well, they upped the offer to six and a half thousand. He's a lucky twat. It's going to cost him £375.20 over five years, that's with all those insurances thrown in, so go out there and break the good news to him. Wendy will then sign him up, so just explain to him what's going on. Then get his insurance for the Golf, cos that's the car he's going home in. We want a cover note faxed here before he goes home.'

'Well Jonathan, looks like you'll be going home in the Golf, is that all right? It's going to cost you £375 per month over five years, are you all right with that? You can say no.'

'That's brill, I wanted that car.'

'So I want you to arrange your insurance, then get the company to fax it to us so you can drive it home. I'll get the log book that will have the make, model, engine size, and colour. I'll also get our fax number for them to fax it to us, I'm going to be gone about fifteen minutes. I have to photocopy some paperwork, so would you like a tea or coffee, Mr Williams?'

'Coffee, please Gordon, white with one sugar.'

'OK, I won't be long, mate.'

Is this bloke thick! I told him how much it's going to cost over five years. He thinks that's OK - £375.20 over five years works out at over twenty-two grand, and he'll be paying that back on an eight grand car, well six grand after the deposit is taken off. Twenty-two thousand pounds - that's how much my first house cost. I had a mortgage for twenty-five years, but the man's happy.

Working in this place can be rather dull, stuck in a room with ten office desks and chairs, and only the phones for company. You can see the outside world through the front and back doors, and the windows in the underwriter's office. So it's pleasant working and walking into that place. The view, as views go, was a pretty picture, with other factories around us, and the south downs in the background, it brightens up the day.

Money transferred to our account, insurance faxed, time to get this man gone.

'So Mr Williams, can you come this way please. We call this the sign-up room. It's another office, but it makes it a bit more private for you. This just takes a couple of minutes. I'll have the car waiting downstairs for you when you've signed up. Wendy will talk you through what you're signing up for.'

All done and dusted, we get the all-clear to release the car. I then lead my customer to his lovely new top-of-his-range V.W Golf, knowing that he's got that car for five years.

'Gordon, thanks for what you've done,' (not a time to feel guilty, he's thanking me for stitching him up. Perhaps he'll give me a back-hander the way he's carrying on).

'You were telling me you're a welder as well, Gordon?'

'That's right, Jonathan, I'm a welder. You see this piece of metal that you're sitting in, I've welded you to this car for five years. So enjoy the car - I know you're going to.'

I hope he never meets the Pope.

21

Take Me to Your Cleaner

In some dealerships, not all, the car cleaner is the most trusted person.

He is the guy who opens up the showroom first thing in the morning, deactivates the alarm, brings the milk in, puts it in the fridge, and does all the salesmen's chores before he sets on about doing his.

Valeter, car cleaner, also used as a driver. Again, one of the important persons on a car site, he sees in the new cars off the transporter, checking the car to make sure that there are no dents, scratches, blemished paint work, just making sure that it's the said car on the paperwork.

The worst thing for any salesman is when your new car arrives without its handbook. No new history service book plus that little booklet of a map of Europe, so if you break down it shows you where you can get help. Yes, that important atlas of countries like Sweden, Russia, and Outer Mongolia. That's annoying when you hand a car over to the customer without those books. The cleaner will not sign for the car, then tell the driver to take it back if he thinks there's something wrong with it.

Then there are the car cleaners who will spend all day preparing one car. You ask them to clean or wipe another vehicle and they think it's an ordeal. 'Can't you see I'm busy,' he will say.

These people are the force that clean every car on site. With their chamois leather and hot bucket of water, off they go and clean those cars on the forecourt, rain, snow, and shine. They make the cars look like new, and once a week they clean the cars in the showroom.

If you have a large dealership, you have two or three car cleaners. Small garages with ten or twelve car size forecourt normally employ a retired man or woman just to wipe the car three times a week. That's it, those people make the cars on the forecourt look like new. When they work in tandem and work as a team, the cars shine in the sun. A good car cleaner is hard to find, so once you find one, you want to keep him or her. They can put value on a car.

The majority of showrooms employ outside companies to do this work. They in turn employ cheap labour just to keep the cost down, so you get a lot of people who can't speak a word of English, working in some prestige car dealerships. So what happens if they can't speak a word of English, how do they get on?

I remember being employed by a company where they only had one person to valet the cars, who nagged his company for help with twenty plus new cars and twenty used cars a week being sold. He needed help big time. His company had no idea what he was doing. They were just happy getting their fee each month. The help they sent was in the form of an Eastern European who, guess what, couldn't speak a word of English.

So one spring morning in May, his helper arrived, and into the showroom he walked.

'I here to help cars.'

'You what?'

'I here to, as he waved his hands, cars.'

'You've lost me, mate.'

In the showroom, Peter our car cleaner was wiping the cars over with a damp cloth. 'I think he's for me,' he shouted. 'I was told I was getting some help today. What is he, Croat?'

'Peter, I really don't know. All I know is, his English is crap.'

'I'm going to have some fun today. I'll take him outside and get him working. Oh mate, you come with me.'

Peter took his helper off to his workshop, which was a garage containing all his cleaning equipment, buffers, vacuum cleaners, polish wax, kettle, teapot, and a radio.

'You understand English?' he asked.

'English?'

'Do you speak any English?'

'English?'

'Don't bother. Take your jacket off and put it on the peg,' he said, pointing to his jacket.

'Jaacket peg.'

'Take your... fuck me, it's going to be a long day this

is, like looking after a deaf dog. Follow me,' beckoning his help to come outside, 'this is a bucket.'

'Bucket.'

'Yer, bucket. We put some water in the bucket like this.' Emptying the contents from his pressure cleaner into the bucket. 'This is hot water. You see the steam?'

'Steam.'

'That's what comes from a train when it goes along the track - Tom the tank. We put cold water in so it's not too hot,' opening the tap that's on the wall. 'Then we get a piece of cowhide, and put it into the water to soften it up. You see these cars - you clean them. I'll show you, OK?'

'OK, show you.'

'You get the bucket with the water, and a cloth like this.'

'Ah cloth.'

'Yer, this is a cloth. You put the cloth into the water, give it a good soaking, like so, take the cloth out, then ring it out like this, twisting the cloth to rid it of excess water.'

'Terwist clooth.'

'Yer, twist it like a chicken's neck, getting all the water out, you bring the cloth to the car.'

'Ah car clooth to car.'

'Watch me, I open the cloth, like so, then go over the car like this, removing any water or dust particles. As you can see, it soaks the dirt and grime up.'

'Crime.'

'Are going to repeat everything I say? What's your name?'

'My name, what's my name?'

'Peter, that's me,' pointing to himself, 'your name?'

'Name, Ivan me Ivan.'

'Ivan, isn't everyone back home in your country called Ivan?'

'Me Ivan.'

'Whatever, you clean this car,' pointing to one next to him, 'like I showed you.'

'Hi Peter. See you got some help at last. You should be able to keep up now.'

Stopping him in his tracks. 'You FUCKING WHAT. They're having a fucking laugh sending me this geek. All I want is to keep you lot off my back. I only want to get on, so they decide to send me a seeker who can't speak a word of fucking English, so how the hell can I get on?'

'Wound you up, have they?'

'Like I was saying, he can't speak a word - what a waste of time.'

I might as well do them myself. I've got twenty odd cars to get ready, some to go into the showroom, the others are going out, plus seventy cars on the forecourt to wipe over. That idiot will have them done by Friday, I can see it. By the time he has done this lot, he'll have to start again, bit like painting the Forth bridge, get to one end and then start again.'

'He'll be all right once he gets the hang of it. He'll be as good as you.'

'I doubt it, Gary. Every time I ask for help, they always send a paraplegic, cheap labour all the time. I don't know how people get away with it, still I've got to play catch-up now.'

'Hi Pete. I see it didn't take long for your new mate to settle in.'

'Why is that, Mick?'

'He's having a fag break.'

'He's only been here, what, five minutes, talk about taking the piss. Where is he? I'm gonna tell him.'

'Oh, you can have a smoke break when you've done those six cars. You've only just started the job.'

'A no cig you say.'

'When you've done at least six cars,' holding up six fingers, then pointing to the cars, 'you can have a cigarette when you have done them.'

The cleaner might as well be talking to himself. He wasn't going to get anywhere with this bloke.

'I'm like a wet nurse looking after a baby, making sure it's all right,' I told my bosses. 'Stop, start, stop, start, is all I'm doing, it's putting me behind. So they send me Ivan who has been cleaning cars for years. Can't you tell he's an expert? He's going to have these cars done today, that's why he needs a break to start. Why couldn't they have sent an English-speaking person? At least I could have said what needed to be done, then let him get on with it.'

'Pete, give the man a couple of days and he will pick up on what to do, you'll see.'

'Mick, I haven't got a few days. I wanted someone who can just walk in and get on with it. All down to profit - paying peanuts, you get monkeys.'

A couple of days later, all seems to be going well. The cars were getting cleaned, Peter was getting on dewaxing the new vehicles, which can takes hours of his time, and his helper was picking up speed. Yes, all was going well... until the day our cleaner was late arriving for work.

Ivan thought he would help by getting the morning up and running for Peter, for when he decided to turn up. We heard he was caught up in traffic. So, moving the sold cars about in the wash area seemed to him a good idea. We let him get on with it.

This was a big mistake. He made the mixture up for the spray to remove the coating that the manufacturer puts on to protect the car from the elements when they're in some compound up or down the country. But, he made the mixture too strong, so when they applied it to the new cars, it burnt into the paint, as well as removing the protective coating. Did the shit hit the fan!

The company lost the contract at the end of the financial year. But we kept on the master car cleaner, Peter. The new people took him on, increased his wages, and gave him a trainee so when he was off, he could trust himself to leave the youngster to do the job without any comeback.

Another tale someone mentioned to me occurred when the driver was out on some errands for the dealership.

A car needed to be returned to the customer after the work had been done, so who else could they call on but the cleaner? The car only had to be delivered a couple of miles away, so, easy enough you would think.

'Fairseat Drive is on the estate just outside of town. I'll give you directions so you don't get lost. You know where Woodlands is?' the aftersales adviser enquired.

'Yes, I've got a few mates who live near there,' the

cleaner replied. 'Will there be anyone in when I get there?'

'No, so just put the keys through the letter box when you park the car, but make sure you lock the car up. Take Diddy with you so he can bring you back. It's all right, I've cleared it with the dwarf so there's no problem with you two going. So leave in about ten minutes, at three o'clock. The car's in the service area. I'll give you the keys when you get changed out of your overalls.'

Now every dealership should have two or three drivers, so if a problem occurs they have a spare driver to deliver the car to its destination with minimum of disruption to the garage.

With having to pay another wage, tax, national insurance, a few dealerships would rather get somebody else to do the job. So you get someone to do all the jobs that need doing, such as picking up the rubbish, washing the windows, going to the post office with the outgoing letters once a day, general dogsbody really.

The customer's house where they had to drop the car off was no more then three miles away, so the drop should take ten minutes at most. Well, for anyone with half a brain. But, when you get two people who are clueless, anything can happen...

'OK, here are the keys. The address is on this piece of paper, so all you have to do is put the keys through the letterbox once you have dropped the car off,' the after-sales adviser told them.

Twenty minutes later, there was a call from one of the cleaners requesting the number of the house where the car was meant to be dropped off. Would someone phone them back with the correct address? Ten minutes, ten to four that afternoon, the cleaners are back having delivered the car. They parked up and got on with their work, cleaning the rest of the cars that needed doing.

A couple of hours later, an irate customer phones asking why her car is parked on a neighbour's drive, and where are the keys to her car?

'Mrs Campbell, let me call you back in five minutes after I find out what the drivers have done to your car?' said a slightly bemused manager. 'Where did you drop that car off?' he asked one of the cleaners.

'Where you told us to drop it off. Why, what's the problem?'

'Well, you put the car on the wrong driveway, and posted the keys through the wrong door.'

'I phoned here and asked for someone from your department to call us back with the house number, but no-one did, so we asked around where this car owner lived. Someone in the road told us the place where we left the car, so that's where we left it.'

'I gave you the address on a slip of paper. What happened to it?'

'You gave me the address, but you didn't give the house number.'

Back in the service reception. 'Did anyone get a message from the cleaners, asking for the house number?' the service manager asked the service personnel that had congregated around the service desk.

'No,' came the reply from the Service receptionist.

'I didn't,' said the other personnel.

Let's give the receptionist a call. 'Hello Joanne, it's Martin down here in the service garage. Did one of the cleaners phone and ask for us to call them back with the house number?'

'Oh yer, I have a note on my desk to give to you. Is it too late to give it to you, this note, Martin?'

'Only by two hours. Thank you, Jo, it's a bit late now.' Down went the phone.

'That fucking stupid woman. She has a note on her desk to give to us that's like two hours too late. Now I've got to phone this Mrs Campbell and explain to her that the driver who left the car didn't have her house number but thought she lived there. This is going to be fun.'

'Hello Mrs Campbell, it's Martin from the garage. The drivers mislaid the paper which had your address on, so they asked someone in your road who thought you lived there where the car is. They posted the keys through that letterbox.'

'Oh dear,' came the reply.

'I take it there is a problem?'

'Slightly.'

'What time are they home tonight?'

'They're not home tonight. They won't be home until Saturday of next week. They've gone away on holiday to the South of France for two weeks. What are you going to do about that? I have no car and it looks like I won't have my car for two weeks.' Then she goes on about how long she has been using the garage, and nothing like this has ever happened to her before.

'Well, shit happens. Do you not have a spare key?'

'I bought the car from your showroom and never got a spare key from them. It just goes to show what type of working place you have there, if no-one knows what's going on and you don't understand each other.

'My car only needed a little work doing on it - a day I was told I'd be without a car - now it looks like two bloody weeks that I will not have a car, so what are you going to do about it?'

'If I can call you back in a couple of minutes, I'll try and sort something out tonight or first thing tomorrow morning, but like I said, give me a moment.'

It was good job that they had a service car spare to loan the lady for the time till she got her keys back.

'If I drive the customer's car, will you follow me in the service loan car, Andy? You can bring me back.' Andy was the cleaner. He removed any grease from the customers' cars once the work had been completed on them. It was a personal touch for the dealership.

'Where are all your drivers? Can't any of them do it, because I'm busy?'

'They are all out delivering cars as you can see. All of these cars need to be delivered by the end of today. Yes, all twenty cars, so you're helping me to drop them off.'

'As if I haven't got enough to do. OK, can we go now then, so I can come back and finish these cars?'

'Let me get the keys then.'

Two minutes later, they were on their way. The service receptionist went first, leading the way, with the cleaner following in the second car. You've heard of the word tailgating? It's dangerous and a risky way of driving, sometimes fatal. In this case, Andy needed to do this just to keep up with the car in front.

Along the twisted roads, like the game of cat and mouse catch me if you can, which he did. He smashed straight in to the back of the car in front. No sooner had the customer's car come out of the bodyshop, than it was time for it to go back in. Back at the garage, they had to call out a pickup truck to bring both cars in to be inspected for the damage they received in their shunt.

The after-sales manager then had to explain his way out of that one to the customer.

The dealership never got a cleaner to drive their customers' cars again.

Working for a small car site, there are normally two salesmen, one of them is senior - the one who will say yes or no in a deal. He also drives the better car, and has the better placed desk so as to be the first to see who walks in.

He also acts as a buyer, with the owner's permission, so if there's a car on the computer screen that someone's selling, he can say we will have that vehicle, and the dealership has bought a car.

So when someone comes into the showroom asking for a specific and precise car, it will be his job to find, with all the auctions and motability sales going on in a week, the required car.

That's exactly what happened. It was a Friday morning when a gentleman came into the showroom wanting to buy a car. There was nothing on the forecourt he liked, so would they mind looking around the country for him, which they did.

They found the car the gentleman required in the raspberry ripples compound, north of the country in Yorkshire, so after going through the details of the car over the phone, and agreeing a price, they decided to purchase the car. The easy part is sitting in front of the computer, reading and answering the questions they supply on the screen. All you do is fill in the boxes of what you want, how many cars you require. If it's one, you put one in the box, and if you want ten, you put in ten. I've heard that when some salesmen leave a company, they have ordered cars in this way so after they've left, a few days later, a car transporter would turn up with five to ten cars which the company never wanted.

So they bought the car over the internet. Then they receive a phone call from the customer asking when he will get his car. They in turn phone the supplier to see when they will be bringing the vehicle to the site, only to be told that they had to make their own arrangements for picking the car up themselves for they had put an X in the wrong box. When reading the order form over again, they saw the box which should have been completed if they required the car to be delivered. It had been left blank.

Being a small site, who were they going to send to fetch it? The cleaner, he can do it. They would pay for him to go to North Yorkshire by train. Now, no disrespect to the cleaner but he was thick as shit and had never in his life been further than Brighton on his holiday. They were sending him to pick the car up. They said they had no choice but to do that. So after checking what time the train departed and arrived, he left the following day. The senior salesman had given instructions about what time he had to call the office. If there were any problems, to call in immediately. Fuck knows what we could do, but it makes people feel important.

Eight hours later, he calls the office to say he's arrived and waiting for a taxi to take him to the compound.

'Go and find yourself a hotel because the car compound closes at five and it's nearly six in the evening. You'll have to get the car in the morning, so enjoy your stay.'

'I don't have any money or a credit card to pay for a hotel. I only have the money for the fuel for the return journey,' came his reply.

'Well, go and find a hotel, then call us back and I'll arrange to pay it for you over the phone.'

Which he did, in the heart of York, so on the phone he got to say what he was doing. The senior salesman gave the receptionist of the hotel his credit card number saying he was paying for the cleaner's evening meal and bed, but not his beverages (bar bill), and could they also arrange a taxi for him in the morning to take him to the compound.

Now the bill was adding up. The train fare, the hotel board, and the petrol for the return journey added up to about one hundred and seventy pounds. To have the car delivered by transporter would have cost one hundred and fifty pounds.

So, after a good cooked meal, plus two bottles of wine and two large brandies which he told them to put on the food bill, he went to bed for the night.

The following morning, with a large full English breakfast inside to keep him going for the day, he waited for the taxi, which came just after nine that morning.

'Been doing the school run,' he explained in a language the cleaner couldn't understand. He just agreed and they set off to the raspberry ripple car compound. Just after ten, the taxi arrives at the compound. He pays the driver, then makes his way to the office to do the paperwork. After twenty minutes he's ready to go home. Then realises he has left the trade plates in the taxi which was waiting at the gate to give them back to him.

'You'll be needing these,' the driver said in a deep Yorkshire accent. He thanked him, placed them on the car, looked at a map to see what was the best way south, then thought that it was going to take hours to get back. Pass Leeds, then on to the M1 heading south towards the M25, but first find the nearest service station and fill the car up.

Back to the car site after a heavy night of rain, the cars looked like they had all been in the safari rally. They were all covered in dust, and nobody to clean them. The two salesmen weren't going to touch them. It wasn't their job. They were waiting for the cleaner to arrive, which he did at eight o'clock that night. The reason and the excuse for the long time to get back, was that he didn't have a pound for the Dartford crossing, so he went anti-clockwise around the M25 putting an extra three hundred miles on the car.

So there it was, the car the customer wanted, the colour, the engine size, the price he was going to pay, all sorted. Taking into account the hotel bill, the cost in petrol, the amount of stone chips it gained from the journey from the north, and the repairs before it left the site, it all came to a tidy sum. The bill for the car, if it had been delivered by the motability delivery transport service, would have come to just under two hundred pounds, with no work to be done on it. The car site's way cost just over three hundred and fifty pounds. Not rocket science to work out the better way.

'Your car's been delivered, so get the cleaners to dewax it. That car should be gone by the weekend,' I was told by my manager.

'Sure, I'll tell my Miss Taylor she can have her car Friday.'

Filling in a cleaning request ticket for the car, all I have to do is put it up on the board in the valeting bay, requesting what day I need it done by, that's all I have to do. With them cleaning the vehicle, I only have to sort the paperwork, and get it insured and taxed. She can drive it away on Friday - easy you might think.

Wrong - the dealership I was working for employed their own car cleaners. They came from Bosnia to escape the horrors of war, which at the time seemed fair. What can you do when the vehicle you're about to hand over has just been ruined?

'It's a bit late to do anything about it now,' the service manager advised me. 'If she doesn't see it, we can get away with it.'

'You what, if she doesn't see it? If she doesn't see that, she shouldn't be fucking driving,' I shouted back at him.

'James, your Miss Taylor is here,' the receptionist informed me.

'On my way.'

'Hello Jean, thanks for coming in at this time of the

day. I can see you're all excited so let's do the paperwork, then you can take this lovely brand new car home.'

When a customer is about to get their brand new car, there is always an element of excitement in the air. Whichever way they paid for the car, it's going to be their pride and joy so you don't want to be the one who ruins it for them.

Once all the paperwork was signed, it was time to take her to the car, then hand it over. Showing her the gears, the lights, the indicators, the spare wheel and the jack, where the oil goes, the dip stick, and the windscreen water bottle, I also tell her, if there are any problems, either phone or bring the car to the service personnel for they will sort her problems out.

Do they hell?

'There you have it, Miss Taylor, it's all yours. The next time you see me is when you bring the car back in either six months or six thousand miles which ever comes first.'

Remember it's a brand new car, so ten minutes after she had driven off, she returned in tears, parked her car, walked into the service area, then started screaming blue murder saying someone had ruined her car, which I knew they had.

What the cleaner had done in his way of wisdom. On the dashboard in the front of the car, the cleaner had used wire wool to remove a sticker from the face on the perspex glass speedometer, causing it to scratch and scuff up so you couldn't read the speed you were going when driving. So when they asked me to calm her down, I said no chance, I'm going home. I didn't fuck her car up.

A friend told me about the time when a cleaner took his time in preparing a car that was going out later that day. Even when the customer was waiting in the showroom, the car still wasn't ready. The car eventually went, but there was one pissed off salesmen.

The following day, the salesman managed to get hold of the cleaner's car keys without him knowing. His scheme was to hide a packet of prawns in the heater system of his car. You know what's going to happen when the winter sets in. When he wants to warm his car up, on one of those frosty mornings, what's going to happen of a night-time. When he parks his car, he'll have cats from miles around sniffing at the smell it's going to let off.

But not all cleaners are thick, you might meet the odd one who can really do a good job. The one who just gets on with his job, causes no problem. Yes, they're the ones who work out of those car parks next to those big supermarkets, who say, 'can I wash your car, need your car washed?' then charge a fiver plus to clean your vehicle.

Then the nice windscreen washers who won't take no for an answer, the ones by those traffic lights, them f-in idiots who get abusive when you tell them no. Especially their wives with their kids strapped to their sides, I say no more.

'Here, have this old business card, give them a call, they're looking for cleaners.'

' Give call, I get job, yes.'

'Whatever.'

Why is it at every main junction around the outskirts of London, when you stop at the traffic lights, these people come out of the woodwork and slap a mop head on your front screen. The soapsuds block your vision, then they expect you to pay them to remove it. When you don't, they tend to get aggressive by booting your car and spitting at you. They always do that when the lights are green and you are moving off, so you can't stop to have a go at them.

I remember going though Brixton, stopping at the junction where the A205 meets the A23, where there was a group of these car windscreen washers waiting to ply their trade. They picked on a transit van and started cleaning the van's windows. The driver was shouting at them to go and multiply somewhere else. Funny, that word is known all around the world, so when he refuses to pay them any money, they started kicking his van.

Then the back door of the transit flew open, a builder jumped out and poured a 4-litre tin of white paint over that person, got back in the van, and drove off to the sound of horns and hooters from the other cars. You can drive past there now without getting any hassle from those people. They must have moved on to somewhere else.

22

A Little Something for the Weekend

What's that saying, 'if it's not broke, don't try and fix it,' so what do some people do?

There was a dealership that was running so smoothly until the day the sales manager got promoted to another site. But as he was dealer principal, the site he left had to employ a sales manager to cover that loss. Someone with a bit of experience knows how to make a profit, keep a happy medium with the sales team that he has there.

Well the showroom found someone they thought filled those requirements. Everything ran like clockwork for the first three weeks, then out of the blue he decided to employ one of his mates who seemed to take over the show. He wanted to get involved with all the deals but he was only a salesman.

Within three weeks, the whole world of this showroom had turned upside down. Two of the sales team members were looking around for other jobs. Sales started to drop.

Nobody wanted to sell cars, well not for the new sales manager and his mate. Everybody resented the pair.

They had a really good salesman who had been with the showroom three and half years. He had been a loyal servant to the dealership, but felt that the mate was muscling in and stopping him from dealing. Every time someone said anything, the reply was, 'I'm just seeing how it's done.'

As the days went by, the new salesman would tell the manager of everything that had taken place on a day-to-day basis, what comments anybody had made about the place, and how it's run. They had a snitch in their midst. If you have a really good salesman, you will try your hardest to make sure he never leaves, so when three salesmen hand their notice in, you start to question why. Well in a normal place you would. Not in this dealership, he didn't. The manager kept it to himself, then put an advert in the local paper, 'Salesmen wanted'.

When the end of the month came, the wage packets arrived on the desks. After studying the contents, one of the team realised some monies were missing, only to be told that it would be put in next month's money - something that's never happened before.

So, as the days drew close to mass exodus, one of the salesmen started having time off, what with the new dealership that he was going to, he was getting ready for the transformation.

Now, some showrooms let you keep your car till your new place of employment sorts you one out, then you hand it back. At least, you're meant to, but when you've really pissed some one off, the last thing he is going to do is put himself out for anyone. Two weeks later, the dealership received a phone call from P&O sea group telling them that they had one of their cars locked up on the Pride of Canterbury, which is a cross-channel ferry from Dover to Calais. When could they come and remove it from their ship, it has been on the ferry for a week now.

The dealer principal went ape shit. He wanted to know why an 18 grand car was sitting on a ferry. Then he wanted to know why three of his top salesmen had left. When he found out why, he went into a bigger rage and sacked the manager there and then, and told him to take his little lap dog with him. He got two of the team back - the third salesman got a manager's job at another dealership - and paid for the other two salesmen to go on a week's holiday, which they took.

I remember a salesman telling me about the time when a bloke came in to the showroom to hire a van. As the story went, they took all the details from the man, photocopied his licence, took the money, and handed the keys over. When you have a car and van hire, you can never be sure who wants a vehicle and what they want to use it for.

Then you get a phone call from H.M. CUSTOMS, telling you that your van is being held in a compound and it's going to cost the company to retrieve it. The van was used to bring tobacco and spirits into the country.

He claimed to have brought back for his own personal use, fifty cases of brandy and 100 kilos of rolling tobacco. Apparently he would have had to have smoked 5 packets of rolling tobacco a day for the next seventy years, that's if he could get up after having drunk two bottles of brandy a day for a year. They wouldn't tell us how much it came to, but quite a few thousand, and a load more.

One story I heard, while having a drink in a refreshment house once, was about a middle-aged man who wanted to hire a vehicle. The only car they had available was a Ford KA which after some deliberation he decided he would take. Sometimes you ask what they're going to use it for. Are they going away for the weekend? A trip to the seaside? Occasionally they make conversation and tell you what they are doing. Some just want the keys and be gone, just like this guy, so after taking a photocopy of his driving licence plus a copy of an address where he was residing, he was on his way after completing the form which records how much petrol is in the tank, any dents etc. Off he went in this lovely Ford 1.3 KA, two-door in blue, paid for in cash.

If you were ever thinking of going to do a bank job, or any other form of hold up, you'd get a fast car like a Jag, a Merc, or a B.M.W, wouldn't you? Not a Ford KA, or a car that's going to break down.

Well, that's what happened to him in this car. It broke down, then had to be towed backed to the garage. Unfortunately for him, the driver noticed he had shotguns in the car so he informed the police, told them where he was going to drop the car off. By the time the tow truck got back to the dealership, the place was swarming with the old bill. They must have got them out of retirement because we didn't think there were that many police in that part of London.

So there was this guy sitting in the car, being towed towards the service area. As soon as the truck stopped and the lorry driver got out, it was like someone had kicked down an anthill. One man, and a few thousand police! Talk about smashing a nut with a sledgehammer. The driver in the KA thought he was in a film shoot, looking a bit bewildered when he was ordered out of the car. He just looked around and carried on talking on his mobile phone. One policeman with a loud hailer kept shouting to the man to get out of the car.

'Are you talking to me?' he said, as he unwound the driver's side window.

'Get out of the car, put your hands above your head,' he was ordered again.

Throwing his mobile phone on to the passenger seat, he got out of the car, sheepishly putting his hands into the air.

'What's the problem?'

'Get on your knees and put your hands behind your head,' he was told.'

'Yer OK, but what's going on?'

With that, two officers ran over to the man. One put what looked like bin ties around his hands, stood him up, then turned him around to face the firing squad. You could smell the stench of crap. This man must have shit himself. Two other officers pulled the guns from the car. Then they started shouting all sorts of questions at him. 'Where were his accomplices? How many in his gang? Where were they targeting?' Talk about Twenty Questions.

It all changed when he shouted he belonged to a gun

club, and was going to the gun club for the afternoon shoot. One of the officers had in his hand his gun licence. That was the reason he wouldn't get out of the vehicle when they asked him to. The other two guns belonged to his colleagues. He looked after their guns in his safe at home.

It was a false alarm. 'You can all stand down,' came the call from a senior officer.

About an hour or so later, when normal life had returned, this guy was still there waiting for a car to pick him up. Needless to say he got his money back for the hire car.